Woody Allen - Filmographie

Zum Buch

2015 ist für Woody Allen ein ganz besonderes Jahr: Am 01. Dezember wird der wohl produktivste Regisseur unserer Zeit 80 Jahre alt. Gleichzeitig begeht er sein 50-jähriges Filmjubiläum:

Mit seiner beispiellosen Kreativität und Vielseitigkeit als Autor, Regisseur, Schauspieler und Musiker hat Woody Allen in 50 Jahren 57 Kinofilme geschaffen, beziehungsweise an ihnen mitgewirkt. Fast jeder kennt den „Stadtneurotiker" oder „Manhattan". Aber wussten Sie auch, dass Woody Allen in einem Film von Jean-Luc Godard mitgespielt hat? Oder dass er einer neurotischen Trickfilm-Ameise seine Stimme lieh?

Zuletzt hatte der Regisseur großen Erfolg mit Filmen wie „Matchpoint" (2005) und den oskarpreisgekrönten Werken „Midnight in Paris" (2011) und „Blue Jasmine" (2013). Aber auch die frühen Woody-Allen-Klassiker lohnen es, in Erinnerung gerufen zu werden. Unvergessen sind Szenen wie die des dauertelefonierenden Tony Roberts in „Mach's noch einmal, Sam" (1972), oder der Fahrstuhl zur Hölle in „Harry Außer Sich" (1997), um nur einige Beispiele zu nennen.

Von „Was gibt's Neues, Pussy?" bis „Irrational Man" finden Sie hier alle Kinofilme von 1965-2015, chronologisch und alphabetisch geordnet, jeweils mit Stab, allen Haupt- und Nebendarstellern und deren Rollen, sowie einem kurzen Handlungsüberblick. Das große alphabetische Register der Darsteller am Ende des Buches ist ein Who is Who aus 50 Jahren Filmgeschichte: Welche prominenten Schauspieler-/innen haben schon eine der heiß begehrten Rollen beim Kultregisseur ergattert? Wessen Karriere begann mit einer nur ganz kleinen Rolle in einem Woody-Allen-Film? Und welche Namen gehören zu den vertrauten Gesichtern, die oft über Jahre die Stammbesetzung der Filme bilden, sei es in den großen, oder nur ganz kleinen Rollen?

Auch die Musik spielt immer eine Hauptrolle beim Klarinettisten Woody Allen. Deshalb werden zu allen Filmen auch die Musiktitel mit Komponisten und Textern genannt. Zusätzlich gibt es eine Zusammenstellung aller Musiktitel, die in mehreren Filmen vorkommen.

Was Sie schon immer über Woody-Allen-Filme wissen wollten – hier, zum Neu- und Wiederentdecken!

Annette Körbel

Woody Allen
Filmographie

Von „What's New Pussycat?" bis „Irrational Man"

1965 - 2015

BoD

Bibliografische Information der Deutschen Nationalbibliothek:
Die Deutsche Nationalbibliothek verzeichnet diese Publikation
in der Deutschen Nationalbibliografie; detaillierte bibliografische
Daten sind im Internet über www.dnb.de abrufbar.

2., aktualisierte Auflage 2015

Herstellung und Verlag:

BoD – Books on Demand, Norderstedt

ISBN **9783735742445**

„Nur er macht uns mit Lachen klüger."

*Vincent über Woody Allen,
in Sophie Lellouches Film „Paris-Manhattan"
(2012)*

Inhalt

I. Die Filme - chronologisch:
   Stab – Darsteller mit ihren Rollen – Handlung – Musik 9

II. Die Filme – alphabetisch: Titel der deutschen Fassung 69

III. Die Filme – alphabetisch: Titel der Originalfassung 71

IV. Musiktitel, die in mehreren Filmen gespielt werden 73

V. Register der Darsteller (Haupt- und Nebendarsteller) 78

I. Die Filme - chronologisch:
Stab – Darsteller mit ihren Rollen – Handlung – Musik

1965

Was Gibt's Neues, Pussy?
(*What's New Pussycat?*)
Frankreich/USA, ca. 104 Minuten

Regie: Clive Donner **Drehbuch:** Woody Allen **Produktion:** Charles K. Feldmann **Kamera:** Jean Badal **Schnitt:** Fergus McDonell **Kostüme:** Gladys de Segonzac **Musik:** Burt Bacharach **Darsteller:** Peter Sellers *(Dr. Fritz Fassbender/Dr. Nikita Popowitsch i. d. dt. Fassung)*; Peter O'Toole *(Michael James)*; Romy Schneider *(Carole Werner)*; Capucine *(Renée)*; Paula Prentiss *(Liz)*; Woddy Allen *(Victor)*; Ursula Andress *(Rita)*; Edra Gale *(Anna Fassbender)*; Katrin Schaake *(Jacqueline)*; Eléonore Hirt *(Mrs. Werner)*; Jean Paredes *(Marcel)*; Jacques Balutin *(Etienne)*; Jess Hahn *(Mr. Werner)*; Howard Vernon *(Arzt)*; Michel Subor *(Philippe)*; Sabine Sun *(Krankenschwester)*; Nicole Karen *(Tempest)*; Jacqueline Fogt *(Charlotte)*; Daniel Emilfork *(Tankstellenwärter)*; Tanya Lopert *(Miss Lewis)*; Barbara Sommers *(Miss Marks)*; Robert Rollis *(Autoverleiher)*; Annette Poivre *(Emma)*; Richard Saint-Bris *(Bürgermeister)*; Marion Conrad/Maggie Wright *(Stripteasetänzerinnen) Ungenannt*[1]: Richard Burton *(Mann in der Stripper Bar)*; Françoise Hardy *(Assistentin des Bürgermeisters)*; Louise Lasser *(Masseuse)*

Handlung: Eine turbulente Komödie um den Casanova Michael, seine Geliebte Carole und einen exzentrischen Psychiater – mit einem bemerkenswerten Staraufgebot.

Musiktitel: Burt Bacharach/Hal David: *What's New Pussycat; Here I Am; Little Red Book; Boston City; Dance Mamma, Dance Pappa, Dance*

1966

Whats's Up, Tiger Lily?
(*What's Up, Tiger Lily?*)
Japan/USA, ca. 77 Minuten

Ungenannt[2]: **Regie:** Senkichi Taniguchi (Original); Woody Allen (Neubearbeitung) **Drehbuch:** Hideo Ando (Original); Woody Allen/Frank Buxton/Len Maxwell/Louise Lasser/Mickey Rose/Julie Bennett/Bryna Wilson (Neubearbeitung) **Produktion:** Tomoyuki Tanaka/Shin Morita (Original); Henri G. Saperstein/Reuben Bercovitch/Woody Allen (Neubearbeitung) **Kamera:** Kazuo Yamada **Schnitt:** Richard Krown **Musik:** The Lovin' Spoonful **Darsteller:** Tatsuya Mihashi *(Agent Phil Moskowitz)*; Akiko Wakabayashi *(Suki Yaki)*; Mie Hama *(Teri Yaki)*; Tadao Nakamaru *(Schäfer Wong)*; Susumu Kurobe *(Wing)*; Sachio Sakai *(Hoodlum)*; Hideyo Amamoto *(Cobra Man)*; Osman Yusuf *(Glücksspieler)*; Tetsu Nakamura *(Außenminister)*; Kumi Mizuno *(Phils Date)*; Woody Allen *(er selbst/Erzähler)*; China Lee *(Stripperin)*; John Sebastian/Zal Yanovsky/Joe Butler/Steve Boone *(sie selbst - The Lovin' Spoonful)*

---

[1] Alle Angaben zu Mitwirkenden, die im Abspann nicht genannt werden, stammen aus der der „Internet Movie Database" (Imdb) www.imdb.com, Stand 15.09.2015

[2] Informationen zu den Mitwirkenden aus: http://www.imdb.com/title/tt0061177/fullcredits?ref_=tt_ql_1, http://www.imdb.com/title/tt0058253/fullcredits?ref_=tt_cl_sm#cast und http://www.djfl.de/entertainment/djfl/1090/109212.html, jeweils Stand 15.09.2015

Handlung: Woody Allen verwandelte für seine erste Regiearbeit einen typischen japanischen Agentenfilm („Kagi No Kagi"/„Schlüssel der Schlüssel") mittels einer neuen, aberwitzigen Synchronisation in eine Persiflage auf das Genre: Agent Phil Moskowitz wird auf die Suche nach dem geheimen Rezept für einen Eiersalat geschickt… In Allens Filmbearbeitung verschwimmen die Grenzen zwischen Parodie und unfreiwilliger Komik des Originals.

1967

Casino Royale
(*Casino Royale*)
UK/USA, ca. 125 Minuten

Regie: John Huston/Kenneth Hughes/Val Guest/Robert Parrish/Joseph McGrath **Drehbuch:** Wolf Mankowitz/John Law/Michael Sayers (sehr frei nach dem gleichnamigen Roman von Ian Fleming) **Produktion:** Charles K. Feldman/Jerry Bresler **Kamera:** Jack Hildyard **Schnitt:** Bill Lenny **Kostüme:** Julie Harris **Musik:** Burt Bacharach **Darsteller:** Peter Sellers (*Evelyn Tremble/James Bond 007*); Ursula Andress (*Vesper Lynd/007*); David Niven (*Sir James Bond*); Orson Welles (*Le Chiffre*); Joanna Pettet (*Mata Bond*); Daliah Lavi (*Die Geheimwaffe*); Woddy Allen (*Jimmy Bond/Dr. Noah*); Deborah Kerr (*Agent Mimi/Lady Fiona*); William Holden (*Ransome*); Charles Boyer (*Le Grand*); John Huston (*McTarry/M*); Kurt Kasznar (*Smernov*); George Raft (*er selbst*); Terence Cooper (*Cooper/James Bond 007*); Barbara Bouchet (*Moneypenny*); Jean-Paul Belmondo (*Französischer Legionär*); Angela Scoular (*Butterblümchen*); Gabriella Licudi (*Eliza*); Tracey Crisp (*Heather*); Elaine Taylor (*Peg*); Jacqueline Bisset (*Miss Langbein*); Alexandra Bastedo (*Meg*); Anna Quayle (*Frau Hoffner*); Derek Nimmo (*Hadley*); Ronnie Corbett (*Paule*); Colin Gordon (*Casino Direktor*); Bernard Cribbins (*Taxifahrer*); Tracy Reed (*Agentin in Schottland*); John Bluthal (*Casino Türsteher*); Geoffrey Bayldon (*Q*); John Wells (*Q's Assistent*); Duncan Macrae (*Inspektor Mathis*); Graham Stark (*Kassierer im Casino*); Chic Murray (*Chic*); Jonathan Routh (*John*); Richard Wattis (*Offizier der brittischen Armee*); Vladek Sheybal (*Le Chiffres Vertreter*); Percy Herbert (*Dudelsackpfeifer*); Penny Riley (*Agentin im Kontrollraum*); Jeanne Roland (*Hauptmann der Garde*); Ungenannt[1]: Geraldine Chaplin (*Keystone Cop*); Peter O'Toole (*Schottischer Dudelsackpfeifer*); Anjelica Huston (*Agent Mimis Hände*)

Handlung: Eine Parodie auf James-Bond-Filme: Sir James Bond wird zu seinem großen Ärger genötigt, seinen Ruhestand zu unterbrechen, denn die Geheimdienstchefs der Großmächte brauchen seine Unterstützung im Kampf gegen eine verbrecherische Organisation, die die Welt bedroht. Um den Gegner zu verwirren, setzt er gleich mehrere Agenten mit Namen „James Bond 007" ein…

Musiktitel: Burt Bacharach/Hal David: *The Look Of Love*; Have No Fear, Bond Is Here* • John Barry: *Born Free* • Claude Debussy: *Suite bergamasque* L75, 3. Satz: *Claire De Lune* • Thomas Augustine Arne: *Rule Brittania*

*In der deutschen Filmfassung wird „The Look Of Love" mit deutschem Text („Ein Blick Von Dir") von Mireille Mathieu gesungen.

1969

Woody, Der Unglücksrabe
(*Take The Money And Run*)
USA, ca. 81 Minuten

Regie: Woody Allen **Drehbuch:** Woody Allen/Mickey Rose **Produktion:** Charles H. Joffe **Kamera:** Lester Shorr **Schnitt:** Paul Jordan/Ron Kalish **Kostüme:** Erick M. Hjemvik **Musik:** Marvin Hamlisch **Darsteller:** Woody Allen *(Virgil Starkwell);* Janet Margolin *(Louise);* Marcel Hillaire *(Fritz);* Jacquelyn Hyde *(Miss Blair);* Lonny Chapman *(Jake);* Jan Merlin *(Al);* James Anderson *(Aufseher der Männer in Ketten);* Jackson Beck *(Erzähler);* Howard Storm *(Fred);* Mark Gordon *(Vince);* Micil Murphy *(Frank);* Minnow Moskowitz *(Joe Agneta);* Nate Jacobson *(Richter);* Grace Bauer *(Farmerin);* Henry Leff *(Vater Starkwell);* Ethel Sokolow *(Mutter Starkwell);* Louise Lasser *(Kay Lewis);* Dan Frazer *(Julius Epstein);* Mike O'Dowd *(Michael Sullivan)* **Ungenannt**[1]: Stanley Ackerman *(Stanley Krim, Amateurfilmer);* Mickey Rose *(Mann in Ketten)*

Handlung: Virgil Starkwell beginnt schon früh eine kriminelle Karriere. Allerdings so ungeschickt, dass er immer wieder im Gefängnis landet. Als er sich in die hübsche Wäscherin Louise verliebt, möchte er ihre gemeinsame Zukunft mit einem Banküberfall sichern… Der Film ist wie eine Dokumentation gestaltet, mit einem Erzähler, eingeblendeten Archivfotos, sowie Kommentaren von Virgil, seiner Familie, Freunden und anderen Wegbegleitern.

Musiktitel: Quincy Jones: *Soul Bossa Nova*

1971

Bananas
(*Bananas*)
USA, ca. 78 Minuten

Regie: Woody Allen **Drehbuch:** Woody Allen/Mickey Rose **Produktion:** Jack Grossberg **Kamera:** Andrew M. Costikyan **Schnitt:** Ralph Rosenblum/Ron Kalish **Kostüme:** Gene Coffin **Musik:** Marvin Hamlisch **Darsteller:** Woody Allen *(Fielding Mellish)*; Louise Lasser *(Nancy)*; Carlos Montalbán *(General Emilio M. Vargas)*; Natividad Abascal *(Yolanda)*; Jacobo Morales *(Esposito)*; Miguel Suárez *(Luis)*; David Ortiz *(Sanchez)*; René Enríquez *(Diaz)*; Jack Axelrod *(Arroyo)*; Roger Grimsby *(er selbst)*; Don Dunphy *(er selbst)*; Martha Greenhouse *(Dr. Feigen)*; Dan Frazer *(Priester)*; Stanley Ackerman *(Dr. Mellish)*; Charlotte Rae *(Mrs. Mellish)*; Howard Cosell *(er selbst)*; Axel Anderson *(Mann im Folterkeller)*; Tigre Pérez *(Pérez)*; Baron De Beer *(Britischer Botschafter)*; Arthur Hughes *(Richter)*; John Braden *(Ankläger)*; Ted Chapman *(Polizist)*; Dorothi Fox *(J. Edgar Hoover)*; Dagne Crane *(Sharon)*; Ed Barth *(Paul)*; Nicholas Saunders *(Douglas)*; Conrad Bain *(Semple)*; Eulogio Peraza *(Dolmetscher)*; Norman Evans *(Senator)*; Robert O'Connel/Robert Dudley *(FBI-Männer)*; Marilyn Hengst *(Norma)*; Ed Crowley/Beeson Carroll *(FBI-Security)*; Allen Garfield *(Mann am Kreuz)*; Princess Fatosh *(Frau mit Schlangenbiss)*; Dick Callinan *(Mann aus der Zigarettenwerbung)*; Hy Anzell *(Patient im OP)* **Ungenannt**[1]: Sylvester Stallone *(Schläger in der U-Bahn)*

Handlung: Der neurotische Produkttester Fielding Mellish hat kein Glück bei den Frauen. Auch seine neueste Eroberung, die politische Aktivistin Nancy, verlässt ihn nach kurzer Zeit wieder. Um ihr zu imponieren, schließt er sich in Südamerika einer Rebellengruppe an und gelangt bald an die Spitze der Revolutionsbewegung…

Musiktitel: Marvin Hamlisch: *Quiero La Noche* • Marvin Hamlisch/Howard Liebling: *Cause I Believe In Loving* • Peter Tschaikowski: *Ouvertüre solennelle 1812* Es-Dur op. 49 • Victor Herbert: *Naughty Marietta*

1972

Was Sie Schon Immer Über Sex Wissen Wollten, Aber Bisher Nicht Zu Fragen Wagten (*Everything You Always Wanted To Know About Sex ... But Were Afraid To Ask*)
USA, ca. 84 Minuten

Regie: Woody Allen **Drehbuch:** Woody Allen (nach dem gleichnamigen Buch von Dr. David Reuben) **Produktion:** Charles H. Joffe **Kamera:** David M. Walsh **Schnitt:** Eric Albertson **Kostüme:** Arnold M. Lipin/G. Fern Weber **Musik:** Mundell Lowe **Darsteller:** Woody Allen (*Hofnarr/Fabrizio/Victor/Spermium*); John Carradine (*Dr. Bernardo*); Lou Jacobi (*Sam*); Louise Lasser (*Gina*); Anthony Quayle (*König*); Tony Randall (*Telefonist*); Lynn Redgrave (*Königin*); Burt Reynolds (*Switchboard*); Gene Wilder (*Dr. Ross*); Jack Barry (*er selbst*); Elaine Giftos (*Mrs. Ross*); Toni Holt (*sie selbst*); Robert Q. Lewis (*er selbst*); Heather MacRae (*Helen*); Pamela Mason (*sie selbst*); Sidney Miller (*George*); Regis Philbin (*er selbst*); Titos Vandis (*Milos*); Stanley Adams (*Bauchchirug*); Oscar Beregi (*Gehirnkontrolleur*); Alan Caillou (*Vater des Hofnarren*); Don Chuy/Tom Mack (*Football Spieler*); Dort Clark (*Sheriff*); Erin Fleming (*das Mädchen*); Geoffrey Holder (*Hexenmeister*); Baruch Lumet (*Rabbi Baumel*); Jay Robinson (*Priester*); Ref Sanchez (*Igor*); Robert Walden (*Spermium*); H.E. West (*Bernard Jaffe*)

Handlung: Ein Episodenfilm als Persiflage auf das gleichnamige, in den USA damals sehr erfolgreiche Buch von Dr. David Reuben und auf die Aufklärungswelle der Zeit.

Die Episoden:

1. Wirken Aphrodisiaka? (*Do Aphrodisiacs Work?*)
2. Was ist Sodomie? (*What Is Sodomy?*)
3. Warum haben manche Frauen Schwierigkeiten, zum Orgasmus zu gelangen? (*Why Do Some Women Have Trouble Reaching An Orgasm?*)
4. Sind Transvestiten Homosexuell? (*Are Transvestites Homosexuals?*)
5. Was Ist Perversion? (*What Are Sex Perverts?*)
6. Sind die Ergebnisse der Ärzte und Kliniken, die Sexualforschung betreiben, genau zutreffend? (*Are The Findings Of Doctors And Clinics Who Do Sexual Research And Experiments Accurate?*)
7. Was Geschieht Bei Der Ejakulation? (*What Happens During Ejaculation?*)

Musiktitel: Cole Porter: *Let's Misbehave* • William Steffe: *Battle Hymn Of The Republic* • James Kerrigen: *Red River Valley*

1972

Mach's Noch Einmal, Sam
(*Play It Again, Sam*)
USA, ca. 85 Minuten

Regie: Herbert Ross **Drehbuch:** Woody Allen **Produktion:** Arthur P. Jacobs **Kamera:** Owen Roizman **Schnitt:** Marion Rothman **Kostüme:** Anna Hill Johnstone **Musik:** Billy Goldenberg/Max Steiner **Darsteller:** Woody Allen *(Allan)*; Diane Keaton *(Linda)*; Tony Roberts *(Dick)*; Jerry Lacy *(Humphrey Bogart)*; Susan Anspach *(Nancy)*; Jennifer Salt *(Sharon)*; Joy Bang *(Julie)*; Viva *(Jennifer)*; Suzanne Zenor *(junge Frau in der Diskothek)*; Diana Davila *(junge Frau im Museum)*; Mari Fletcher *(Phantasie-Sharon)*; Michael Greene *(1. Rowdy)*; Ted Markland *(2. Rowdy)*

Handlung: Der Filmkritiker und Kinofreak Allan wird von seiner Frau verlassen. Alle Versuche seiner Freunde Linda und Dick ihn zu verkuppeln bleiben erfolglos. Aber auch Frauenheld Humphrey Bogart mischt sich ein…

Musiktitel: Oscar Peterson: *Blues For Alan Felix* • Max Steiner: *Casablanca* • Herman Hupfeld: *As Time Goes By* • Claude Joseph Rouget de Lisle: *La Marseillaise*

1973

Der Schläfer
(*Sleeper*)
USA, ca. 84 Minuten s/w

Regie: Woody Allen **Drehbuch:** Woody Allen/Marshall Brickman **Produktion:** Jack Grossberg **Kamera:** David M. Walsh **Schnitt:** Ralph Rosenblum **Kostüme:** Joel Schumacher **Musik:** Woody Allen mit The Preservation Hall Jazz Band/The New Orleans Funeral Ragtime Orchestra **Darsteller:** Woody Allen *(Miles Monroe)*; Diane Keaton *(Luna Schlosser)*; John Beck *(Erno Windt)*; Mary Gregory *(Dr. Melik)*; John McLiam *(Dr. Agon)*; Bartlett Robinson *(Dr. Orva)*; Don Keefer *(Dr. Tryon)*; Brian Avery *(Herald Cohen)*; Chris Forbes *(Rainer Krebs)*; Peter Hobbs *(Dr. Dean)*; Susan Miller *(Ellen Pogrebin)*; Spencer Milligan *(Jeb Hrmthmg)*; Lou Picetti *(M.C.)*; Jessica Rains *(Frau im Spiegel)*; Stanley Ross *(Sears Swiggles)*; Marya Small *(Dr. Nero)*

Handlung: Eine Science-Fiction-Film-Parodie: Miles wird irrtümlich nach einer OP eingefroren, wacht erst 200 Jahre später wieder auf und findet sich in einem totalitären Staat wieder…

Musiktitel: Richard A. Whiting/Raymond B. Egan: *Till We Meet Again* • Walter Donaldson/Gus Kahn: *Yes Sir, That's My Baby* • Irving Berlin: *A Pretty Girl Is Like A Melody* • King Oliver: *Canal Street Blues*

1975

Die Letzte Nacht Des Boris Gruschenko
(*Love And Death*)
Frankreich/USA, ca. 81 Minuten

Regie: Woody Allen **Drehbuch:** Woody Allen **Produktion:** Charles H. Joffe **Kamera:** Ghislain Cloquet **Schnitt:** Ralph Rosenblum **Kostüme:** Gladys De Segonzac **Musik:** Sergei Prokofjew **Darsteller:** Woody Allen *(Boris Gruschenko)*; Diane Keaton *(Sonja)*; Harold Gould *(Anton)*; Olga Georges-Picot *(Gräfin Alexandrovna)*; Zvee Scooler *(Vater)*; Despo Diamantidou *(Mutter);* Sol Frieder *(Voskovec)*; Jessica Harper *(Natasha)*; Lloyd Battista *(Don Francisco)*; Alfred Lutter III *(Junger Boris)*; Georges Adet *(Nehamkin)*; Frank Adu *(Drill Sergeant)*; Edmond Ardisson *(Priester)*; Féodor Atkine *(Mikhail)*; Albert Augier *(Kellner)*; Yves Barsaco *(Rimsky)*; Jack Berard *(General Lecoq)*; Eva Bertrand *(Frau im „Hygiene-Spiel")*; George Birt *(Arzt)*; Yves Brainville *(Andre)*; Gerard Buhr *(Diener)*; Brian Coburn *(Dimitri)*; Henri Coutet *(Minskov)*; Patricia Crown/Narcissa McKinley *(Cheerleader)*; Henry Czarniak *(Ivan)*; Sandor Eles *(Soldat 2)*; Luce Fabiole *(Großmutter)*; Florian *(Onkel Nikolai)*; Jacqueline Fogt *(Ludmilla)*; Harry Hankin *(Onkel Sasha)*; Tony Jay *(Vladimir Maximovitch)*; Tutte Lemkow *(Pierre)*; Jack Lenoir *(Krapotkin)*; Leib Lensky *(Pfarrer Andre)*; Anne Lonnberg *(Olga)*; Roger Lumont *(1. Bäcker)*; Ed Marcus *(Raskov)*; Jacques Maury *(Second)*; Aubrey Morris *(Soldat 4)*; Denise Peron *(Spanische Gräfin)*; Beth Porter *(Anna)*; Alan Rossett *(Wache)*; Shimen Ruskin *(Borslov)*; Percival Russel *(Berdykov)*; Chris Sanders *(Joseph)*; C.A.R. Smith *(Pfarrer Nikolai)*; Fred Smith *(Soldat)*; Bernard Taylor *(Soldat 3)*; Clément Thierry *(Jacques)*; Alan Tilvern *(Sergeant)*; James Tolkan *(Napoleon)*; Helene Vallier *(Madame Wolfe)*; Howard Vernon *(General Leveque)*; Glenn Williams *(Soldat 1)*; Jacob Witkin *(Sushkin)* **Ungenannt**[1]: Norman Rose *(Tod, Stimme)*

Handlung: Liebe in Zeiten des Krieges: Boris ist unglücklich in seine Cousine Sonja verliebt. Obwohl für den Militärdienst denkbar ungeeignet, muss er in den Krieg ziehen, wo er zum unfreiwilligen Helden wird. In der Zwischenzeit hat Sonja einen anderen geheiratet. Doch die Wege der beiden kreuzen sich wieder…

> *„Der Originaltitel ‚Love and Death' erinnert in seiner entwaffnenden Schlichtheit nicht von ungefähr an ‚War and Peace': […] Marx Brothers und Karamasov Brothers standen gleichermaßen Pate bei dieser schwarzen Farce […]. Intelligent demontiert der militante Pazifist Woody Allen das erhabene Pathos von Hollywoods historischen Epen. Wo, bitte, geht's zur Front?"*[3]

Musiktitel: Sergei Prokofjew: *Suite* op. 60, aus dem Film *Leutnant Kishe*; *Kantate* op. 78, aus dem Film *Alexander Newski*; *Suite* op. 33, aus der Oper *Die Liebe Zu Den Drei Orangen* • Luigi Boccherini: *Streichquintett E*-Dur op. 13 Nr. 5 • Wolfgang Amadeus Mozart: *Ouvertüre* zur Oper *Die Zauberflöte* KV 620

---

[3] Filmtips In: Die Zeit 38/1975

1976

Der Strohmann
(*The Front*)
USA, ca. 91 Minuten

Regie: Martin Ritt **Drehbuch:** Walter Bernstein **Produktion:** Martin Ritt **Kamera:** Michael Chapman **Schnitt:** Sidney Levin **Kostüme:** Ruth Morley **Musik:** Dave Grusin **Darsteller:** Woody Allen *(Howard Prince)*; Zero Mostel *(Hecky Brown)*; Herschel Bernardi *(Phil Sussman)*; Michael Murphy *(Alfred Miller)*; Andrea Marcovicci *(Florence Barrett)*; Lloyd Gough *(Delaney)*; Joshua Shelley *(Sam);* Remak Ramsay *(Hennessey)*; Marvin Lichterman *(Myer Prince)*; David Margulies *(Phelps)*; Norman Rose *(Howards Anwalt)*; Charles Kimbrough *(Ausschussberater)*; Josef Sommer *(Vorsitzender des Komitees)*; Danny Aiello *(Danny LaGattuta)*; Georgann Johnson *(TV-Moderatorin)*; Scott McKay *(Hampton)*; David Clarke *(Hubert Jackson)*; I.W. Klein *(Bankangestellter)*; John Bentley *(Barkeeper)*; Julie Garfield *(Margo)*; Murray Moston *(Boss)*; McIntyre Dixon *(Harry Stone)*; Rudolph Wilrich *(Tailman)*; Burt Britton *(Buchhändler)*; Albert Ottenheimer *(Schuldirektor)*; William Bogert *(Parks)*; Joey Faye *(Kellner)*; Marilyn Sokol *(Sandy)*; John J. Slater *(Fernsehdirektor)*; Renée Paris *(Mädchen in Hotel Lobby)*; Gino Gennaro *(Bühnenarbeiter)*; Joan Porter *(Myers Ehefrau)*; Andrew Bernstein/Jacob Bernstein *(Alfreds Kinder)*; Matthew Tobin/Sam McMurray *(Partygäste)*; Marilyn Persky *(His Date)*; Joe Jamrog/Michael Miller *(FBI-Männer)*; Lucy Lee Flippin *(Krankenschwester)*; Jack Davidson/Donald Symington *(Kongressabgeordneter)*; Patrick McNamara *(Federal Marshal)*

Handlung: Der Film spielt in den USA zur Zeit der McCarthy-Ära: Restaurant-Kassierer Howard Prince ist ständig in Geldnot. Doch dann trifft er seinen alten Schulfreund Alfred Miller wieder, einen Drehbuchautor, der vom „Komitee für unamerikanische Umtriebe" mit Berufsverbot belegt wurde. Miller überredet Howard, als Strohmann für sich und andere arbeitslose Schriftsteller zu arbeiten und deren Drehbücher als seine eigenen auszugeben… Regisseur und Drehbuchautor des Films standen ebenso wie einige der mitwirkenden Schauspieler in den 50er Jahren selber auf der sogenannten „schwarzen Liste".

Musiktitel: Johnny Richards/Carolyn Leigh: *Young At Heart; Come On Daisy* • Carrie Hoffman/Ira Gassman: *Anything For A Laugh*

1977

Der Stadtneurotiker
(*Annie Hall*)
USA, ca. 89 Minuten

Regie: Woody Allen **Drehbuch:** Woody Allen/Marshall Brickman **Produktion:** Charles H. Joffe **Kamera:** Gordon Willis **Schnitt:** Ralph Rosenblum **Kostüme:** Ruth Morley **Musik:** s. Musiktitel **Darsteller:** Woody Allen *(Alvy Singer)*; Diane Keaton *(Annie Hall)*; Tony Roberts *(Rob)*; Carol Kane *(Allison)*; Paul Simon *(Tony Lacey)*; Shelley Duvall *(Pam)*; Janet Margolin *(Robin)*; Christopher Walken *(Duane Hall)*; Colleen Dewhurst *(Annies Mutter)*; Mordecai Lawner *(Alvys Vater)*; Joan Neuman *(Alvys Mutter)*; Jonathan Munk *(Alvy als Kind)*; Christine Jones *(Dorrie)*; Donald Symington *(Annies Vater)*; John Glover *(Schauspieler-Ex-Freund von Annie)*; Russell Horton *(Mann in der Kinoschlange)*; Mary Boylan *(Miss Reed)*; Marshall McLuhan *(er selbst)*; Helen Ludlam *(Oma Hall)*; Ruth Volner *(Alvys Tante)*; Martin Rosenblatt *(Alvys Onkel)*; Hy Anzell *(Joey Nicholas)*; Rashel Novikoff *(Tante Tessie)*; Wendy Girard *(Janet)*; John Doumanian *(Kokser)*; Bob Maroff/Rick Petrucelli *(Männer vor dem Kino)*; Lee Callahan *(Kartenverkäufer im Kino)*; Chris Gampel *(Arzt)*; Dick Cavett *(er selbst)*; Mark Lenard *(Marine Offizier)*; Dan Ruskin *(Komiker bei der Wahlparty)*; Bernie Styles *(Agent des Komikers)*; Johnny Haymer *(Komiker)*; Ved Bandhu *(Maharishi)*; John Dennis Johnston *(L. A. Polizist)*; Lauri Bird *(Tony Lacey's Freundin)*; Jim McKrell/Jeff Goldblum/William Callaway/Roger Newman/Alan Landers/Jean Sarah Frost *(Partygäste)*; Vince O'Brien *(Hotelarzt)*; Humphrey Davis *(Alvis Psychiater)*; Veronica Radburn *(Annies Psychiaterin)*; Robin Mary Paris/Charles Levin *(Schauspieler bei der Probe)*; Wayne Carson *(Inspizient)*; Michael Karm *(Probenleiter)*; Petronia Johnson/Shaun Casey *(Tonys Dates im Nachtlokal)*; Riccardo Bertoni/Michael Aronin *(Kellner im Nachtlokal)*; Lou Picetti/Loretta Tupper/James Burge/Shelley Hack/Albert Ottenheimer/Paula Trueman *(Fremde auf der Straße)*; Beverly D'Angelo/Tracey Walter *(Schauspieler in Robs Fernsehshow)*; David Wier/Keith Dentice/Susan Mellinger/Hamit Perezic/James Balter/Eric Gould/Amy Levitan *(Alvys Klassenkammeraden)*; Gary Allen/Frank Vohs/Sybil Bowan/Margaretta Warwick *(Lehrer)*; Lucy Lee Flippin/Gary Mule Deer *(Kellner im vegetarischen Restaurant)*; Sigourney Weaver *(Alvys Date vor dem Kino)*; Walter Bernstein *(Annies Date vor dem Kino)*

Handlung: Eine Beziehungskomödie über ein neurotisches Paar im New York der 70er Jahre: Nachdem sich Komiker Alvy Singer und seine Freundin Annie Hall getrennt haben, lässt Alvy die gemeinsame Zeit Revue passieren und versucht zu verstehen, warum es zur Trennung kommen musste. Dabei gehen seine Erinnerungen auch in die Kindheit zurück…

Musiktitel: Carmen Lombardo/John Loeb: *Seems Like Old Times* • Isham Jones/Gus Kahn: *It Had To Be You* • Tim Weisberg: *A Hard Way To Go* • Weihnachtslieder: *Christmas Medley* • Eric Coates/Jack Lawrence: *Sleepy Lagoon* • Wolfgang Amadeus Mozart: *Sinfonie Nr. 41 (Jupiter-Sinfonie) C*-Dur KV 551, 4. *Molto allegro*

1978

Innenleben
(*Interiors*)
USA, ca. 88 Minuten

Regie: Woody Allen **Drehbuch:** Woody Allen **Produktion:** Charles H. Joffe **Kamera:** Gordon Willis **Schnitt:** Ralph Rosenblum **Kostüme:** Joel Schumacher **Musik:** s. Musiktitel **Darsteller:** Kristin Griffith *(Flyn)*; Mary Beth Hurt *(Joey)*; Richard Jordan *(Frederick)*; Diane Keaton *(Renata)*; E. G. Marshall *(Arthur)*; Geraldine Page *(Eve)*; Maureen Stapleton *(Pearl)*; Sam Waterston *(Mike)*; Missy Hope *(Joey als Kind)*; Kerry Duffy *(Renata als Kind)*; Nancy Collins *(Flyn als Kind)*; Penny Gaston *(Eve als Kind)*; Roger Morden *(Arthur als Kind)*; Henderson Forsythe *(Judge Bartel)*

Handlung: Das erste Filmdrama von Woody Allen und eine Hommage an den schwedischen Regisseur Ingmar Bergman: Nachdem Rechtsanwalt Arthur seiner Familie eröffnet hat, dass er sich, zunächst vorübergehend, von seiner Ehefrau, der Innenarchitektin Eve, trennen wird, gerät auch das Leben der drei erwachsenen Töchter aus den Fugen…

Musiktitel: Fats Waller/Andy Razaf: *Keepin' Out Of Mischief Now* • Jelly Roll Morton: *Wolverine Blues*

1979

Manhattan
(*Manhattan*)
USA, ca. 92 Minuten s/w Breitbandformat

Regie: Woody Allen **Drehbuch:** Woody Allen/Marshall Brickman **Produktion:** Charles H. Joffe **Kamera:** Gordon Willis **Schnitt:** Susan E. Morse **Kostüme:** Albert Wolsky **Musik:** George Gershwin **Darsteller:** Woody Allen *(Isaac)*; Diane Keaton *(Mary)*; Michael Murphy *(Yale)*; Mariel Hemingway *(Tracy)*; Meryl Streep *(Jill)*; Anne Byrne *(Emily)*; Karen Ludwig *(Connie)*; Michael O'Donoghue *(Dennis)*; Victor Truro/Tisa Farrow/Helen Hanft *(Party Gäste)*; Bella Abzug *(Ehrengast)*; Gary Weis *(TV-Direktor)*; Kenny Vance *(TV-Produzent)*; Charles Levin/Karen Allen/David Rasche *(TV-Schauspieler)*; Damion Sheller *(Ikes Sohn)*; Wallace Shawn *(Jeremiah)*; Mary Linn Baker/Frances Conroy *(Shakespeare Schauspieler)*; Bill Anthony/John Doumanian *(Porschebesitzer)*; Raymond Serra *(Kellner in der Pizzeria)*

Handlung: Im Leben des Autors Isaac läuft es weder beruflich noch privat rund: Er kündigt überstürzt seinen Job beim Fernsehen, die lesbische Ex-Frau plant die Veröffentlichung peinlicher Details aus dem gemeinsamen Eheleben, und seine Beziehung zur erst 17-jährigen Tracy nimmt er nicht wirklich ernst. Richtig kompliziert wird es aber, als er Tracy verlässt, um ausgerechnet ein Verhältnis mit der Geliebten seines besten Freundes zu beginnen… Der Film ist zugleich eine Liebeserklärung an New York: „*New York was his town, and it always would be.*" (Woody Allen in „Manhattan")

Musiktitel: George Gershwin: *Rhapsody In Blue; Love Is Sweeping The Country; Land Of The Gay Caballero; Sweet And Low Down; I've Got A Crush On You; Do-Do-Do; S'Wonderful; Oh, Lady Be Good; Strike Up The Band; Embraceable You; Someone To Watch Over Me; He Loves, And She Loves; But Not For Me* • Wolfgang Amadeus Mozart: *Sinfonie Nr. 40 g-Moll KV 550, 1. Molto allegro*

1980

Stardust Memories
(*Stardust Memories*)
USA, ca. 88 Minuten s/w

Regie: Woody Allen **Drehbuch:** Woody Allen **Produktion:** Robert Greenhut **Kamera:** Gordon Willis **Schnitt:** Susan E. Morse **Kostüme:** Santo Loquasto **Musik:** Dick Hyman **Darsteller:** Woody Allen (*Sandy Bates*); Charlotte Rampling (*Dorrie*); Jessica Harper (*Daisy*); Marie-Christine Barrault (*Isobel*); Tony Roberts (*Tony*); Helen Hanft (*Vivian Orkin*); John Rothman (*Jack Abel*); Anne DeSalvo (*Sandys Schwester*); David Lipman (*Sandys Chauffeur*); Joan Neuman (*Sandys Mutter*); Eli Mintz (*Alter Mann*); Daniel Stern (*Schauspieler*); Amy Wright (*Shelley*); Gabrielle Strasun (*Charlotte Ames*); Bob Maroff (*Jerry Abraham*); Leonardo Cimino (*Sandys Analytiker*); Robert Munk (*Sandy als Kind*); Ken Chapin (*Sandys Vater*); Jaqui Safra (*Sam*); Sharon Stone (*junge Frau im Zug*); Andy Albeck/Robert Friedman/Douglas Ireland/Jack Rollins (*Studiobosse*); Howard Kissel (*Sandys Manager*); Max Leavitt (*Sandys Arzt*); Renée Lippin (*Sandys Presseagent*); Sol Lomita (*Sandys Steuerberater*); Irving Metzman (*Sandys Anwalt*); Dorothy Leon (*Sandys Köchin*); Roy Brocksmith (*Dick Lobel*); Simon Newey (*Mr. Payson*); Victoria Zussin (*Mrs. Payson*); Frances Pole (*Libby*); Bill Anthony/Filomena Spagnuolo/Ruth Rugoff/Martha Whitehead (*Fans bei Ankunft im Hotel*); Judith Roberts (*Sängerin*); Barry Weiss (*Tänzer*); Robin Ruinsky/Adrian Richards/Dominick Petrolino/Sharon Brous/Michael Zannella/Doris Dugan Slater/Michael Goldstein/Neil Napolitan (*Fragensteller bei Filmvorführung*); Stanley Ackerman (*Reporter*); Noel Behn (*Doug Orkin*); Candy Loving (*Tonys Freundin*); Denice Danon/Sally Demay/Tom Dennis/Edward S. Kotkin/Laura Delano/Lisa Friedman/Brent Spiner/Gardenia Cole/Maurice Shrog/Larry Robert Carr/Brian Zoldessy/Melissa Slade/Paula Raflo/Jordan Derwin/Tony Azito/Marc Murray/Helen Hale/Carl Don/Victoria Page/Bert Michaels/Deborah Johnson (*Fans in der Lobby*); Benjamin Rayson (*Dr. Paul Pearlstein*); Mary Mims (*Claire Schaeffer*); Charles Lowe (*Varieté-Sänger*); Marie Lane (*Cabaretsängerin*); Gustave Tassell/Marina Schiano/Dimitri Vassilopoulos/Judith Crist/Carmin Mastrin (*Cabaretbesucher*); Sylvia Davis (*Agressionsopfer*); Joseph Summo (*Agressor*); Victor Truro (*Psychoanalytiker im „Aggressions-Film"*); Irwin Keyes/Bonnie Hellman/Patrick Daly/Joe Pagano/Wayne Maxwell/Ann Freeman/Bob Miranti (*Fans vor dem Hotel*); Cindy Gibb/Manuella Machado (*junge Fans*); Judith Cohen/Madeline Moroff/Maureen P. Levins (*Freundinnen von Sandys Schwester*); E. Brian Dean (*Polizist*); Marvin Peisner (*Ed Rich*); Robert Tennenhouse/Leslie Smith/Samuel Chodorov (*Autogrammjäger auf der Strandpromenade*); Philip Lenkowsky (*Autogrammjäger/Attentäter*); Vanina Holasek (*Isobels Tochter*); Michel Touchard (*Isobels Sohn*); Kenny Vance/Iryn Steinfink (*Neue Studiobosse*); Frank Modell (*Textumschreiber*); Anne Korzen/Eric Van Valkenburg (*Frau und Mann in Eisdiele*); Susan Ginsburg (*Platzanweiserin*); Ostaro (*Astrologe*); Wade Barnes/Gabriel Barre/Charles Riggs III/Geoffrey Riggs/Martha Sherrill/Ann Risley/Jade Bari/Marc Geller/Daniel Friedman/James Otis/Judy Goldner/Rebecca Wright/Perry Gewertz/Larry Fishman/Liz Albrecht/Sloane Bosniak/James Harter/Henry House/Largo Woodruff/Jerry Tov Greenberg/Mohammid Nabi Kiani (*UFO-Anhänger*); Alice Spivak (*Krankenschwester*); Armin Shimerman/Edith Grossman/Jacqueline French (*Zuhörer bei Laudatio*); John Doumanian (*armenischer Fan*); Jack Hollander (*Polizist, der Sandy verhaftet*) *Ungenannt*[1]: Louise Lasser (*Sekretärin von Sandy Bates*)

Handlung: Regisseur Sandy Bates reist zu einem Filmkunstwochenende, wo er im Hotel Stardust mit einer Retrospektive seiner Filme geehrt werden soll. Wenn er nicht gerade von seinen zahlreichen Fans belagert wird, hält er melancholische Rückschau auf sein Leben, insbesondere auf sein Liebesleben. Dabei mischen sich immer wieder Ausschnitte aus seinen Filmen mit tatsächlichen Begebenheiten. Der erfolgsverwöhnte Bates, der für seine Komödien geliebt wird, aber am liebsten nur noch Tragödien drehen würde, erweist sich als ein Mensch mit tiefgreifenden Zweifeln und Ängsten... Der Film ist thematisch an Fellinis „8 ½" angelehnt.

Musiktitel: Dick Hyman: *Hebrew School Rag* • Cole Porter: *Just One Of Those Things; Easy To Love* • Sidney Bechet: *Tropical Mood Meringue* • Gus Kahn/Isham Jones: *I'll See You In My Dreams* • Lester Young: *Tickletoe* • Bert Kalmer/Harry Ruby: *Three Little Words* • Ary Barroso/S.K. Russell: *Brazil* • J. Russel Robinson/Con Conrad: *Palesteena* • Edward Heyman/Robert Sour/Johnny Green/Frank Eyton: *Body And Soul* • Modest Mussorgski: *Eine Nacht Auf Dem Kahlen Berg* • Irving Mills/Edgar Sampson/Benny Goodman: *If Dreams Come True* • Count Basie: *One O'Clock Jump* • Maceo Pinkard/Sidney Milton: *Sugar* • Ben Bernie/Kenneth Casey/Maceo Pinkard: *Sweet Georgia Brown* • Glenn Miller: *Moonlight Serenade* • Hoagy Carmichael/Mitchell Parish: *Stardust*

1982

Eine Sommernachts-Sexkomödie
(*A Midsummer Night's Sex Comedy*)
USA, ca. 84 Minuten

Regie: Woody Allen **Drehbuch:** Woody Allen **Produktion:** Robert Greenhut **Kamera:** Gordon Willis **Schnitt:** Susan E. Morse **Kostüme:** Santo Loquasto **Musik:** Felix Mendelssohn-Bartholdy **Darsteller:** Woody Allen (*Andrew*); Mia Farrow (*Ariel*); José Ferrer (*Leopold*); Julie Hagerty (*Dulcy*); Tony Roberts (*Maxwell*); Mary Steenburgen (*Adrian*); Adam Redfield (*Student Foxx*); Moishe Rosenfeld (*Mr. Hayes*); Thimothy Jenkins (*Mr. Thomson*); Michael Higgins (*Reynolds*); Sol Frieder (*Carstairs*); Boris Zoubok (*Purvis*); Thomas Barbour (*Blint*); Kate McGregor-Stewart (*Mrs. Baker*)

Handlung: New York um 1900, zu einer Zeit, als „*es noch keine Reparaturwerkstätten des Doktor Freud [gab], weshalb man entweder an Geister glaubte [...] oder an den Brettern der Beziehungskiste rüttelte [...]*:[4] Andrew Hobbs und seine Frau Adrian laden Freunde zum Wochenende in ihr Landhaus ein, und schon beginnt eine Komödie um die Liebeswirren zwischen 3 Paaren, inspiriert von Shakespeares „Sommernachtstraum", Ingmar Bergmans „Lächeln einer Sommernacht", möglicherweise auch von Jean Renoirs „Landpartie".

Musiktitel: Felix Mendelssohn-Bartholdy: *Hochzeitsmarsch*, aus *Ein Sommernachtstraum* op. 61 Nr. 7; *Sinfonie Nr. 3 a-Moll (Schottische)* op. 56; *Violinkonzert e-Moll* op. 64; *Klavierkonzert* Nr. 2 d-Moll op. 40; *Ouvertüre* zu *Ein Sommernachtstraum* E-Dur op. 21 • Franz Schubert: *Wohin*, aus dem Liederzyklus *Die Schöne Müllerin* op. 25 Nr. 2 (D 795) • Robert Schumann: *Ich Grolle Nicht*, aus *Dichterliebe* op. 48 Nr. 7 • Albert Hay Malotte: *The Lord's Prayer*

---

[4] Hellmuth Karasek: Gute, alte Zeit. In: Der Spiegel 43/1982

1983

Zelig
(*Zelig*)
USA, ca. 76 Minuten s/w und Farbe

Regie: Woody Allen **Drehbuch:** Woody Allen **Produktion:** Robert Greenhut **Kamera:** Gordon Willis **Schnitt:** Susan E. Morse **Kostüme:** Santo Loquasto **Musik:** Dick Hyman **Darsteller:** Woody Allen (*Leonard Zelig*); Mia Farrow (*Dr. Eudora Fletcher*); Patrick Horgan (*Erzähler*); Garrett Brown (*Schauspieler-Zelig*); Stephanie Farrow (*Dr. Fletchers Schwester Meryl*); Will Holt (*Kanzler bei Massenveranstaltung*); Sol Lomita (*Martin Geist*); John Rothman (*Paul Deghuee*); Deborah Rush (*Lita Fox*); Marianne Tatum (*Schauspielerin-Fletcher*); Mary Louise Wilson (*Zeligs Halbschwester Ruth*); John Buckwalter (*Dr. Sindell*); Marvin Chatinover/Stanley Swerdlow (*Diagnose-Ärzte*); Paul Nevens (*Dr. Birsky*); Howard Erskine (*Arzt mit Injektionsspritze*); George Hamlin (*Experimentelle-Drogen-Arzt*); Ralph Bell/Richard A. Whiting/Will Hussong (*andere Ärzte*); Robert Iglesia (*Mann beim Friseur*); Eli Resnick (*Mann im Park*); Edward McPhillips (*Schotte*); Gale Hansen/Michael Jeter (*Studenten*); Peter McRobbie (*Sprecher bei Arbeiterversammlung*); Alice Beardsley (*Telefonvermittlerin*); Paula Trueman (*Frau am Telefon*); Ed Lane (*Mann am Telefon*); Charles Denney (*Schauspieler-Arzt*); Michael Kell (*Schauspieler-Koslow*); Sharon Ferrol (*Miss Baker*); Richard Litt (*Charles Koslow*); Dimitri Vassilopoulos (*Martinez*); Francis Beggins (*City Hall Speaker*); Jean Trowbridge (*Dr. Fletchers Mutter*); Ken Chapin (*Interviewer*); Gerald Klein/Vincent Jerosa (*Hearst Gäste*); Stanley Simmonds (*Litas Anwalt*); Robert Berger (*Zeligs Anwalt*); Jeanine Jackson (*Helen Gray*); Erma Campbell (*Zeligs Frau*); Anton Marco/Louise Deitch (*Opfer von Zelig*); Bernice Dowis (*verunglimpfende Frau*); John Doumanian (*Griechischer Kellner*); Bernie Herold (*Carter Dean*); Susan Sontag (*sie selbst*); Irving Howe (*er selbst*); Saul Bellow (*er selbst*); Bricktop (*er selbst*); Dr. Bruno Bettelheim (*er selbst*); Prof. John Morton Blum (*er selbst*); Marshall Coles, Sr. (*Calvin Turner*); Ellen Garrison (*Ältere Dr. Fletcher*); Jack Cannon (*Mike Geibell*); Theodore R. Smits (*Ted Bierbauer*); Sherman Loud (*Älterer Paul Deghuee*); Elizabeth Rothschild (*Ältere Schwester Meryl*); Kuno Sponholz (*Oswald Pohl*); Ed Herlihy (*Ansager - Pathe News*); Dwight Weist (*Ansager - Hearst Metrotone*); Gordon Gould (*Radioansager*); Windy Craig (*Ansager - Universal Wochenschau*); Jurgen Kuehn (*Ansager - Deutsche U.F.A. Wochenschau*)

Handlung: Der Film erzählt die Geschichte von Leonard Zelig, der in den 20er und 30er Jahren Aufsehen erregt. Er leidet nämlich an krankhafter Überanpassung, ist gewissermaßen ein menschliches Chamäleon: So nimmt er neben einem Indianer das Äußere eines Indianers an, unter Gangstern wird er selber zu einem Gangster. Als medizinisches Phänomen wird er zunächst von Arzt zu Arzt gereicht, bis sich schließlich die Psychologin Dr. Eudora Fletcher seiner annimmt und sich in ihn verliebt… Der Film wurde in Form einer Dokumentation gedreht, wobei Allens Figuren zum Teil so perfekt in echten Wochenschauaufnahmen aufgehen, dass sie wie reale Personen des Zeitgeschehens erscheinen.

Musiktitel: Dick Hyman: *Leonard The Lizard*; *Doin' The Chameleon*; *Chameleon Days*; *You May Be Six People, But I Love You*; *Reptile Eyes*; *The Changing Man Concerto* • Harry Link/Billy Rose/Fats Waller: *I've Got A Feeling I'm Falling* • Ray Henderson/Sam M. Lewis/Joe Young: *I'm Sitting On Top Of The World*; *Five Feet Two, Eyes Of Blue* • Raymond B. Egan/Gus Kahn/Richard A. Whiting: *Ain't We Got Fun* • Lew Brown/B. G. DeSylva/Ray Henderson: *Sunny Side Up* • Fred E. Ahlert/Roy Turk: *I'll Get By* • Bud Green/Harry Warren: *I Love My Baby, My Baby Loves Me* • A.H. Gibbs/Joe Grey/Leo Wood: *Runnin' Wild* • John Loeb/Carmen Lombardo: *A Sailboat In The Moonlight* • James P. Johnson/Cecil Mack: *Charleston* • Fred Fisher: *Chicago* • George D. Lottman/Alfred H. Miles/Domenico Sanino/Charles A. Zimmerman: *Anchors Aweigh* • Albert von Tilzer: *Take Me Out To The Ballgame* • Pierre Degeyter: *Die Internationale*

1984

Broadway Danny Rose
(*Broadway Danny Rose*)
USA, ca. 81 Minuten

Regie: Woody Allen **Drehbuch:** Woody Allen **Produktion:** Robert Greenhut **Kamera:** Gordon Willis **Schnitt:** Susan E. Morse **Kostüme:** Jeffrey Kurland **Musik:** Dick Hyman/Nick Apollo Forte **Darsteller:** Woody Allen (*Danny Rose*); Mia Farrow (*Tina Vitale*); Nick Apollo Forte (*Lou Canova*); Corbett Monica (*er selbst*); Howard Storm (*er selbst*); Morty Gunty (*er selbst*); Will Jordan (*er selbst*); Jackie Gayle (*er selbst*); Jack Rollins (*er selbst*); Sandy Baron (*er selbst*); Paul Greco (*Vito Rispoli*); Frank Renzulli (*Joe Rispoli*); Olga Barbato (*Angelina*); Edwin Bordo (*Johnny Rispoli*); Peter Castellotti (*Ganove in der Lagerhalle*); Craig Vandenburgh (*Ray Webb*); Herb Reynolds (*Barney Dunn*); Gerald Schoenfeld (*Sid Bacharach*); Sandy Richman (*Teresa*); Gina DeAngelis (*Johnnys Mutter*); Milton Berle (*er selbst*); David Kissell (*Phil Chomsky*); Gloria Parker (*Wasserglas-Virtuosin*); Bob Rollins/Etta Rollins (*Luftballonfigurenmacher*); Bob Weil (*Herbie Jayson*); David Kieserman (*Ralph, Clubbesitzer*); Mark Hardwick (*Blinder Xylophonist*); Alba Ballard (*Vogelfrau*); Maurice Shrog (*Hypnotiseur*); Belle Berger (*Frau in Trance*); Herschel Rosen (*Ehemann der Frau*); Joe Franklin (*er selbst*); Cecilia Amerling (*Fan in der Garderobe*); Maggie Ranone (*Lous Tochter*); Charles D'Amodio (*Lous Sohn*); Joie Gallo (*Angelinas Assistentin*); Carl Pistilli (*Tommys Bruder*); Lucy Iacono (*Tommys Mutter*); Julia Barbuto (*Frau mit tropischen Fischen*); Anna Sceusa (*Frau bei Angelina*); Nicholas Pantano/Rocco Pantano (*Begrüßer bei der Party*); Tony Turca (*Rocco*); Gilda Torterello (*Annie*); Ronald Maccone (*Vincent*); Antoinette Raffone (*Vincents Frau*); Michael Badalucco/Richard Lanzano (*Männer, die Geldscheine zerreißen*); Dom Matteo (*Carmine*); Camille Saviola/Sheila Bond/Betty Rosotti (*Partygäste*); Howard Cosell (*er selbst*); John Doumanian (*Waldorf Manager*); Gary Reynolds (*Freund des Managers*); Diane Zolten/William Paulson/George Axler (*Fans im Waldorf*); Leo Steiner (*Delibesitzer*)

Handlung: Künstleragent Danny Rose tut viel für seine Schützlinge, auch für die schwierigsten Fälle legt er sich ins Zeug. Trotzdem verlassen die Künstler ihn meist, sobald sich der Erfolg einstellt. Eines Tages bietet sich die Chance, Schlagersänger Lou Canova zum großen Comeback zu verhelfen. Wäre da nur nicht die Mafia…

Musiktitel: Nick Apollo Forte: *Agita*; *My Bambina* • Luigi Denza: *Funiculi, Funicula* • Charles Ward: *The Band Played On* • Cole Porter: *All Of You*; *Begin The Beguine* • Russ Morgan/Larry Stock/James Cavanaugh: *You're Nobody Till Somebody Loves You* • Ernesto de Curtis: *Torna A Surriento*

1985

The Purple Rose Of Cairo
(*The Purple Rose Of Cairo*)
USA, ca. 79 Minuten

Regie: Woody Allen **Drehbuch:** Woody Allen **Produktion:** Robert Greenhut **Kamera:** Gordon Willis **Schnitt:** Susan E. Morse **Kostüme:** Jeffrey Kurland **Musik:** Dick Hyman **Darsteller:** Mia Farrow (*Cecilia*); Jeff Daniels (*Tom Baxter/Gil Shepherd/*); Danny Aiello (*Monk*); Dianne Wiest (*Emma*); Van Johnson (*Larry*); Zoe Caldwell (*Die Gräfin*); John Wood (*Jason*); Milo O'Shea (*Pfarrer Donnelly*); Deborah Rush (*Rita*); Irving Metzman (*Kinodirektor*); John Rothman (*Mr. Hirschs Anwalt*); Stephanie Farrow (*Cecilias Schwester*); Alexander Cohen (*Raoul Hirsch*); Camille Saviola (*Olga*); Karen Akers (*Kitty Haynes*); Michael Tucker (*Gils Agent*); Annie-Joe Edwards (*Delilah*); Peter McRobbie (*Der Kommunist*); Juliana Donald (*Platzanweiserin*); Edward Herrmann (*Henry*); David Kieserman (*Restaurant-Chef*); Elaine Grollman/Victoria Zussin/Mark Hammond/Wade Barnes/Joseph G. Graham/Don Quigley/Maurice Brenner (*Restaurantgäste*); Milton Seaman/Mimi Weddell (*Ticketkäufer*); Tom Degidon (*Ticketabreißer*); Mary Hedahl (*Popcornverkäuferin*); Paul Herman/Rick Petrucelli/Peter Castellotti (*Münzwerfer*); Eugene Anthony (*Arturo*); Ebb Miller (*Bandleader*); Margaret Thompson/George Hamlin/Helen Hanft/Leo Postrel/Helen Miller/George Martin/Crystal Field (*Kinozuschauer*); Ken Chapin/Robert Trebor (*Reporter*); Benjamin Rayson/Jean Shevlin/Albert S. Bennett/Martha Sherrill/Gretchen MacLane/Edwin Bordo (*Kinogänger*); Andrew Murphy/Thomas Kubiak (*Polizisten*); Raymond Serra (*Hollywood Manager*); George Manos (*Presseagent*); David Tice (*Kellner*); James Lynch (*Oberkellner*); Sydney A. Blake (*Varieté-Reporter*); Peter Von Berg (*Drogeriekunde*); David Weber (*Foto-Double*); Glenne Headley/Willie Tjan/Lela Ivey/Drinda La Lumia (*Prostituierte*); Loretta Tupper (*Musikladenbesitzerin*)

Handlung: New Jersey zur Zeit der Depression: Die Kellnerin Cecilia flüchtet vor ihrem tristen Job und den Problemen mit ihrem Ehemann so oft es geht ins Kino. Besonders der Hollywoodstar Gil Shepherd, Darsteller des Tom Baxter im Film „The Purple Rose of Cairo" hat es ihr angetan. Eines Tages spricht Tom Baxter sie von der Leinwand aus direkt an, um dann ganz aus dem Film heraus und in ihr Leben zu treten. Dies bereitet nicht nur den Hollywoodproduzenten Probleme...

Musiktitel: Irving Berlin: *Cheek To Cheek* • Dick Hyman: *One Day At A Time* • Bud Green/Harry Warren: *I Love My Baby, My Baby Loves Me* • Ray Henderson: *Alabamy Bound*

1986

Hannah Und Ihre Schwestern
(*Hannah And Her Sisters*)
USA, ca. 103 Minuten

Regie: Woody Allen **Drehbuch:** Woody Allen **Produktion:** Robert Greenhut **Kamera:** Carlo Di Palma **Schnitt:** Susan E. Morse **Kostüme:** Jeffrey Kurland **Musik:** s. Musiktitel
Darsteller: Woody Allen (*Mickey*); Michael Caine (*Elliot*); Mia Farrow (*Hannah*); Carrie Fisher (*April*); Barbara Hershey (*Lee*); Lloyd Nolan (*Evan*); Maureen O'Sullivan (*Norma*); Daniel Stern (*Dusty*); Max von Sydow (*Frederick*); Dianne Wiest (*Holly*); Julie Kavner (*Gail*); Bobby Short (*er selbst*); Joanna Gleason (*Carol*); Lewis Black (*Paul*); Julia Louis-Dreyfus (*Mary*); Christian Clemenson (*Larry*); J. T. Walsh (*Ed Smythe*); John Turturro (*Autor*); Rusty Magee (*Ron*); Allen DeCheser/Artie DeCheser (*Hannahs Zwillinge*); Ira Wheeler (*Dr. Abel*); Richard Jenkins (*Dr. Wilkes*); Tracy Kennedy (*Brunch Gast*); Fred Melamed (*Dr. Grey*); Benno Schmidt (*Dr. Smith*); Maria Chiara (*Manon Lescaut*); Stephen de Fluiter (*Dr. Brooks*); The 39 Steps (*Rock Band*); Rob Scott (*Drummer*); Beverly Peer (*Bassist*); Daisy Previn/Moses Farrow (*Hannahs Kinder*); Paul Bates (*Theaterdirektor*); Carrotte/Mary Pappas (*Theaterangestellte*); Bernie Leighton (*Pianist beim Vorsingen*); Ken Costigan (*Pfarrer Flynn*); Helen Miller (*Mickeys Mutter*); Leo Postrel (*Mickeys Vater*); Susan Gordon-Clark (*Kellnerin*); William Sturgis (*Elliots Analytiker*); Daniel Haber (*Krishna*); Verna O. Hobson (*Mavis*); John Doumanian/Fletcher Farrow Previn/Irwin Tenenbaum/Amy Greenhill/Dickson Shaw/Marje Sheridan (*Thanksgiving Gäste*); Ivan Kronenfeld (*Lees Ehemann*) **Ungenannt**[1]: Soon-Yi Previn (*Thanksgiving Gast*); Tony Roberts (*Norman, Mickeys Ex-Partner*); Sam Waterston (*David*)

Handlung: Im Zentrum dieses vielschichtigen Films stehen die drei Schwestern Hannah, Lee und Holly, Töchter eines Künstlerpaares und ebenfalls künstlerisch ambitioniert: Hannah, der ruhende Pol der Familie, ist eine erfolgreiche Schauspielerin, Ehefrau und Mutter. Lee ist unglücklich mit dem misanthropischen Künstler Frederick verheiratet, während Holly, immer noch Single, bisher vergeblich versuchte, als Schauspielerin Fuß zu fassen. Bei einem Thanksgiving-Fest verliebt sich Hannahs Ehemann Elliot in Lee, so dass auch Hannahs heile Welt zu zerbrechen droht. Als die Familie zwei Jahre später wieder an Thanksgiving zusammen kommt, hat sich vieles verändert. Daran ist auch Mickey, der hypochondrische Ex-Mann von Hannah nicht ganz unschuldig…

Musiktitel: Joseph McCarthy/James v. Monaco: *You Made Me Love You* • Sammy Cahn/Jule Styne: *I've Heard That Song Before* • Richard Rodgers/Lorenz Hart: *Bewitched; Where or When; You Are Too Beautiful; Isn't It Romantic* • Johann Sebastian Bach: *Konzert für 2 Violinen und Orchester d-Moll BWV 1043; Cembalokonzert f-Moll BWV 1056* • Frank Foster/Count Basie: *Back To The Apple* • Giacomo Puccini: aus der Oper *Madame Butterfly; Sola, perduta, abbandonata,* aus der Oper *Manon Lescaut* • Raymond Klages/Jesse Greer: *Just You, Just Me* • Benny Carter: *The Trot* • Johnny Mercer/Victor Schertzinger: *I Remember You* • Jimmy Campbell/Reg Connelly/Ted Shapiro: *If I Had You* • Cole Porter: *I'm In Love Again* • Jerome Kern/Johnny Mercer: *I'm Old Fashioned* • Jerome Kern/Dorothy Fields: *The Way You Look Tonight* • Johnny Burke/Jimmy Van Heusen: *It Could Happen To You; Polkadots And Moonbeams* • Vincent Rose/Al Jolson/B. G. DeSylva: *Avalon* • Michael Bramon: *Slip Into the Crowd* • Harry Ruby: *Freedonia's Going To War* aus „*Die Marx Brothers Im Krieg*"

1987

Radio Days
(*Radio Days*)
USA, ca. 85 Minuten

Regie: Woody Allen **Drehbuch:** Woody Allen **Produktion:** Robert Greenhut **Kamera:** Carlo Di Palma **Schnitt:** Susan E. Morse **Kostüme:** Jeffrey Kurland **Musik:** Dick Hyman **Darsteller:** Danny Aiello (*Rocco*); Jeff Daniels (*Biff Baxter*); Mia Farrow (*Sally White*); Seth Green (*Joe*); Robert Joy (*Fred*); Julie Kavner (*Mutter*); Diane Keaton (*Neujahrssängerin*); Julie Kurnitz (*Irene*); Renée Lippin (*Ceil*); Kenneth Mars (*Rabbi Baumel*); Josh Mostel (*Abe*); Tony Roberts (*Silver-Dollar-Conférencier*); Wallace Shawn (*Maskierter Rächer*); Michael Tucker (*Vater*); David Warrilow (*Roger*); Dianne Wiest (*Bea*); Mike Starr/Paul Herman (*Einbrecher*); Don Pardo (*Moderator von „Guess That Tune"*); Martin Rosenblatt (*Mr. Needleman*); Helen Miller (*Mrs. Needleman*); Danielle Ferland (*Kinderstar*); Michael Murray (*Gauner aus dem „Maskierten Rächer"*); William Flanagan (*„Maskierter-Rächer"-Ansager*); William Magerman (*Großvater*); Leah Carrey (*Großmutter*); Joy Newman (*Ruthie*); Hy Anzell (*Mr. Waldbaum*); Judith Malina (*Mrs. Waldbaum*); Fletcher Farrow Previn (*Andrew*); Oliver Block (*Nick*); Maurice Toueg (*Dave*); Sal Tuminello (*Burt*); Rebecca Nickels (*Evelyn Goorwitz*); Mindy Morgenstern (*Lehrerin „Zeigen und Erzählen"*); David Mosberg (*Arnold*); Ross Morgenstern (*Ross*); Andrew Clark (*Sidney Manulis*); Lee Erwin (*Rollschuhbahn-Organist*); Roger Hammer (*Richard*); Terry Lee Swarts/Margaret Thomson (*Nachtklubbesucher*); Tito Puente (*Latino Bandleader*); Denise Dummont (*Latino Sängerin*); Dimitri Vassilopoulos (*Porfirio*); Larry David (*kommunistischer Nachbar*); Rebecca Schaeffer (*Tochter des Kommunisten*); Belle Berger (*Mrs. Silverman*); Guy Le Bow (*Bill Kern*); Brian Mannain (*Kirby Kyle*); Stan Burns (*Bauchredner*); Todd Field (*Schlagersänger*); Peter Lombard (*Abercrombie-Gastgeber*); Martin Sherman (*Mr. Abercrombie*); Crystal Field/Maurice Shrog (*Abercrombie-Paar*); Marc Colner (*Wunderkind*); Roberta Bennett (*Lehrerin mit Karotte*); Joel Eidelsberg (*Mr. Zipsky*); Peter Castellotti (*Mr. Davis*); Gina DeAngelis (*Rocco's Mutter*); Shelley Delaney (*Tschechow-Schauspielerin*); Dwight Weist (*Angriff-auf-Pearl-Harbor-Ansager*); Ken Levinsky/Ray Marchica (*USO Musiker*); J. R. Horne (*Biff-Baxter-Ansager*); Kuno Sponholz (*Deutscher*); Henry Yuk (*Japaner*); Sydney A. Blake (*Miss Gordon*); Kitty Carlisle Hart (*Radio Sängerin*); Henry Cowen (*Schuldirektor*); Philip Shultz (*Pfeifer*); Mercedes Ruehl/Bruce Jarchow (*Werbeagenten*); Greg Gerard (*Songschreiber*); David Cale (*Regisseur*); Ira Wheeler (*Sponsor*); Hannah Rabinowitz (*Frau des Sponsors*); Edward S. Kotkin (*Sprachlehrer*); Ruby Payne/Jaqui Safra (*Sprachstudenten*); Paul Berman (*„Gay-White-Way"-Ansager*); Richard Portnow (*Sy*); Barbara Gallo/Jane Jarvis/Liz Vochecowizc (*Tanzpalast Musiker*); Ivan Kronenfeld (*Vor Ort Reporter*); Frank O'Brien (*Feuerwehrmann*); Yolanda Childress (*Pollys Mutter*); Artie Butler (*Neujahrs Bandleader*); Gregg Almquist/Jackson Beck/Wendell Craig/W. H. Macy/Ken Roberts/Norman Rose/Kenneth Welsh (*Radiostimmen*) **Ungenannt**[1]: Woody Allen (*Erzähler*); Fred Melamed (*Bradley*)

Handlung: Geschichten rund ums Radio und ein nostalgischer Rückblick auf seine große Zeit: Im Zentrum des Films steht der Junge Joe, der in den 30er und 40er Jahren mit seiner Großfamilie im New Yorker Stadtteil Queens aufwächst. Das Radio ist aus dem Alltag der Menschen nicht wegzudenken. Jeder hat seine Lieblingssendung und ganz persönliche Erinnerungen, die damit verbunden sind. Und dann ist da noch die junge Sally White, die von einer glamourösen Karriere beim Rundfunk träumt...

Musiktitel: Nikolai Rimski-Korsakow: *Hummelflug* • Arthur Schwartz/Howard Dietz: *Dancing In The Dark* • William Jerome/Jean Schwartz: *Chinatown, My Chinatown* • Robert Hargreaves/Stanley J. Damerell/Tolchard Evans: *Let's All Sing Like The Birdies Sing* • Kurt Weill/Maxwell Anderson: *September Song,* aus dem Musical „*Knickerbocker Holiday*" • Edward Hyman/Robert Sour/Johnny Green/Frank Eyton: *Body And Soul* • Joe Garland: *In The Mood* • Dick Hyman: *Radio Show Themes*; *Re-Lax Jingle* • Jimmy Eaton/Terry Shand: *I Double Dare You* • Harry Warren/Al Dubin: *You're Getting To Be A Habit With Me*; *Lullaby Of Broadway* • Matos Rodríguez: *La Cumparsita* • Vincent Youmans/Gus Kahn: *Carioca* • Zequinha Abreu/Aloysio Oliveira: *Tico Tico* • Cole Porter: *Begin The Beguine*; *Just One Of Those Things*; *You'd Be So Nice To Come Home To*; *Night and Day* • Sy Oliver: *Opus One* • A. Domínguez: *Frenesi* • Jack Lawrence/Arthur Altman: *All Or Nothing At All* • Herbert Stothart/Rudolf Friml: *The Donkey Serenade* • Meredith Willson: *You And I* • Johnny S. Black: *Paper Doll* • Al Dexter: *Pistol Packin' Mama* • Al Dubin/Jimmy McHugh: *South American Way* • Milton Drake/Al Hoffman/Jerry Livingston: *Mairzy Doats* • Moe Jaffe/Jack Fulton/Nat Bonx: *If You Are But A Dream* • Jack Lawrence: *If I Didn't Care* • Jule Styne/Frank Loesser: *I Don't Want To Walk Without You* • Sammy Kaye/Don Reid: *Remember Pearl Harbor* • Margarita Lecuona/S.K. Russel: *Babalu* • Arthur Schwartz/Frank Loesser: *They're Either Too Young Or Too Old* • Lew Brown/Sammy Fain: *That Old Feeling* • Walter Kent/Nat Burton: *The White Cliffs Of Dover* • Gordon Jenkins: *Goodbye* • Ned Washington/George Bassman: *I'm Getting Sentimental Over You* • F.W. Meacham: *American Patrol* • Billy Strayhorn: *Take The A' Train* • Harry Warren/Mack Gordon: *You'll Never Know* • Xavier Cugat/Al Stillman: *One, Two, Three, Kick*

1987

September
(*September*)
USA, ca. 79 Minuten

Regie: Woody Allen **Drehbuch:** Woody Allen **Produktion:** Robert Greenhut **Kamera:** Carlo Di Palma **Schnitt:** Susan E. Morse **Kostüme:** Jeffrey Kurland **Musik:** s. Musiktitel
Darsteller: Denholm Elliott (*Howard*); Mia Farrow (*Lane*); Elaine Stritch (*Diane*); Jack Warden (*Lloyd*); Sam Waterston (*Peter*); Dianne Wiest (*Stephanie*); Ira Wheeler (*Mr. Raines*); Jane Cecil (*Mrs. Raines*); Rosemary Murphy (*Mrs. Mason*)

Handlung: Lane hat nach einem Selbstmordversuch den Sommer in ihrem Landhaus in Vermont verbracht und plant ihre Rückkehr nach New York. Ihre Freundin Stephanie ist bei ihr. Überraschend reist auch Lanes Mutter Diane, eine ehemalige Schauspielerin, mit ihrem Mann an. Diane lädt zum Wochenende zusätzlich die Nachbarn Peter und Howard ein, und schon bald kommt es nicht nur zu romantischen Verwicklungen, auch ein altes Familiengeheimnis wird gelüftet…

Musiktitel: Frank Loesser: *On A Slow Boat To China* • Johnny Green/Edward Heyman: *Out Of Nowhere* • Sam Coslow/Arthur Johnston: *Just One More Chance* • Leo Robin/Richard A. Whiting/Newell Chase: *My Ideal* • Irving Berlin: *What'll I Do* • Jerome Kern/Otto Harbach/Oscar Hammerstein II: *Who* • Al J. Neiburg/Doc Daugherty/Ellis Reynolds: *I'm Confessin'* • Will Hudson/Irving Mills/Eddie DeLange: *Moonglow* • Robert Katscher/B.G. De Sylva: *When Day Is Done* • Cole Porter: *Night And Day*

1987

King Lear
(*King Lear*)
F, ca. 87 Minuten

Regie: Jean Luc Godard **Drehbuch:** Jean Luc Godard **Produktion:** Yoram Globus/ Menahem Golan/Tom Luddy **Kamera:** Sophie Maintigneux **Schnitt:** Jean-Luc Godard
Darsteller: *Ungenannt*[1]: Woody Allen (*Mr. Alien*); Freddy Buache (*Professor Quentin*); Léos Carax (*Edgar*); Julie Delpy (*Virginia*); Jean-Luc Godard (*Prof. Pluggy*); Suzanne Lanza (*Rolle ungenannt*); Kate Mailer (*sie selbst*); Norman Mailer (*er selbst*); Burgess Meredith (*Don Learo*); Michèle Pétin (*Journalist*); Molly Ringwald (*Cordelia*); Peter Sellars (*William Shakespeare Junior der Fünfte*)

Handlung: Ein formal unkonventioneller Film, der mit der gleichnamigen Tragödie von Shakespeare nicht viel zu tun hat: Nach dem Reaktorunfall von Tschernobyl gibt es nur wenige Überlebende. Einer davon ist William Shakespeare Junior der Fünfte. Er hat den Auftrag, das kulturelle Erbe seines Vorfahren für die Menschheit zu retten… Zu Beginn des Films hört man die Aufzeichnung eines Telefonates: Der Produzent Menahem Golan drängt Godard, den Film, der in Cannes vorgestellt werden soll, endlich zu vollenden. Und so wird „[…] *aus dem Film ein Possenspiel über die Tiefschläge, die ihn verhindert haben.*"[5] Woody Allen verkörpert in einer kleinen Rolle den Cutter „Mr. Alien".

---
[5] Zeitmosaik In: Die Zeit 23/1987

1988

Eine Andere Frau
(*Another Woman*)
USA, ca. 78 Minuten

Regie: Woody Allen **Drehbuch:** Woody Allen **Produktion:** Robert Greenhut **Kamera:** Sven Nykvist **Schnitt:** Susan E. Morse **Kostüme:** Jeffrey Kurland **Musik:** s. Musiktitel
Darsteller: Philip Bosco (*Sam*); Betty Buckley (*Kathy*); Blythe Danner (*Lydia*); Sandy Dennis (*Claire*); Mia Farrow (*Hope*); Gene Hackman (*Larry*); Ian Holm (*Ken*); John Houseman (*Marions Vater*); Martha Plimpton (*Laura*); Gena Rowlands (*Marion Post*); David Ogden Stiers (*Vater der jungen Marion*); Harris Yulin (*Paul*); Frances Conroy (*Lynn*); Fred Melamed (*Stimme des Patienten*); Kenneth Welsh (*Donald*); Bruce Jay Friedman (*Mark*); Bernie Leighton (*Klavierspieler*); Jack Gelber/Paul Sills/John Schenck (*Gäste der Geburtstagsparty*); Noel Behn/Gretchen Dahm/Janet Frank/Dana Ivey/Fred Melamed/Alice Spivak (*Gäste der Verlobunsgfeier*); Mary Laslo (*Clara*); Carol Schultz (*junge Clara*); Dax Munna (*kleiner Paul*); Heather Sullivan (*kleine Marion*); Margaret Marx (*junge Marion*); Jennifer Lynn McComb (*junge Claire*); Caroline McGee (*Marions Mutter*); Stephen Mailer (*junger Paul*); Jacques Levy (*Jack*); Dee Dee Friedman (*Kellnerin*); Josh Hamilton (*Lauras Freund*); Kathryn Grody (*Cynthia*); John Madden Towey (*Kellner*); Michael Kirby (*Psychiater*); Fred Sweda (*Tom Banks*); Jill Whitaker (*Eleanor Banks*)

Handlung: Die Philosophieprofessorin Marion Post hat sich in ein Appartement zurückgezogen, um in Ruhe ihr Buch zu Ende zu schreiben. Dort wird sie durch einen Luftschacht unfreiwillig Zeugin von Gesprächen, die der benachbarte Psychologe mit seinen Patienten führt. Schließlich weckt eine junge, schwangere Frau mit ihren Sorgen und Ängsten Marions Interesse und sie beginnt, ihr eigenes Leben zu überdenken… „Eine Andere Frau" ist der erste einer Reihe von Filmen, die Woody Allen mit Ingmar Bergmans bevorzugtem Kameramann Sven Nykvist drehte.

Musiktitel: Erik Satie: *Gymnopédie Nr. 3* • Kurt Weill/Bertolt Brecht: *Bilbao Song*, aus dem Musical *Happy End* • Johann Sebastian Bach: *Suite Nr. 6 für Violoncello Solo D-Dur BWV 1012; Sonaten für Violoncello und Klavier* Nr. 2 D-Dur und Nr. 3 g-Moll BWV 1028/1029 • Edgard Varèse: *Ecuatorial* • Juan Tizol: *Perdido* • Cole Porter: *You'd Be So Nice To Come Home To* • Jerome Kern/Dorothy Fields/Jimmy McHugh: *Lovely To Look At* • Jerome Kern/Dorothy Fields: *A Fine Romance* • Jerome Kern/Oscar Hammerstein II: *Make Believe* • Gustav Mahler: *Sinfonie Nr. 4 G-Dur* • J. Will Callahan/Lee S. Roberts: *Smiles* • Jimmy McHugh/Dorothy Fields: *On The Sunny Side Of The Street* • Fred E. Weatherly/Haydn Wood: *Roses Of Picardy*

1989

New Yorker Geschichten
(*New York Stories*)
USA, ca. 119 Minuten

Drei Kurzfilme von drei verschiedenen Regisseuren (Scorsese/Coppola/Allen):

1. Lebensstudien (*Life Lessons*)

Regie: Martin Scorsese **Drehbuch:** Richard Price **Produktion:** Barbara DeFina **Kamera:** Nestor Almendros **Schnitt:** Thelma Schoonmaker **Kostüme:** John Dunn **Musik:** s. Musiktitel **Darsteller:** Nick Nolte (*Lionel Dobie*); Rosanna Arquette (*Paulette*); Patrick O'Neal (*Phillip Fowler*); Steve Buscemi (*Gregory Stark*): Phil Harper (*Geschäftsmann*); Peter Gabriel (*er selbst*)

Handlung: Der erfolgreiche Maler Lionel Dobie gerät, nicht zum ersten Mal, kurz vor einer wichtigen Ausstellung in eine Krise. Dazu kommt, dass er hoffnungslos in die Kunststudentin Paulette verliebt ist, die seine Gefühle aber nicht erwidert…

Musiktitel: Keith Reid/Gary Brooker: *Whiter Shade Of Pale*; *Conquistador* • Jack Bruce/Peter Brown: *Politician* • Nappy Brown/Ozzie Cadena/Lew Herman: *The Right Time* • Bob Dylan: *Like A Rolling Stone* • Johnny Burke/Jimmy Van Heusen: *It Could Happen To You* • Johnny Mercer/Herold Arlen: *That Old Black Magic* • Ned Washington/Victor Young: *Stella By Starlight* • Giacomo Puccini: *Nessun dorma,* aus der Oper *Turandot* • Nick Christian Sayer: *Sex Kick* • Cole Porter: *What Is This Thing Called Love?* • Django Reinhardt: *Bolero De Django*

2. Leben Ohne Zoe (*Life Without Zoe*)

Regie: Francis Ford Coppola **Drehbuch:** Francis Ford Coppola/Sofia Coppola **Produktion:** Fred Roos/Fred Fuchs **Kamera:** Vittorio Storaro **Schnitt:** Barry Malkin **Kostüme:** Sofia Coppola **Musik:** Carmine Coppola/Kid Creole and the Coconuts **Darsteller:** Adrien Brody (*Mel*); Giancarlo Giannini (*Claudio*); James Keane (*Jimmy*); Heather McComb (*Zoe*); Jenny Nichols (*Lundy*); Don Novello (*Hector*); Talia Shire (*Charlotte*)

Handlung: Die 12-jährige Zoe lebt alleine mit ihrem Butler in einem Hotel, da ihre Eltern, der Flötist Claudio und die Fotografin Charlotte, ständig unterwegs sind. Bei allem Luxus ist sie doch einsam, und versucht daher ihre Eltern, die sich voneinander entfremdet haben, wieder zusammen zu bringen…

Musiktitel: August Darnell: *Zoe*; *Daiquiri Daiquira*; *Schoolin'*; *Abu*; *The Robbery*; *People Will Talk*; *Party Girl*; *Don't Lead Me On*; *March Of The Waiters*; *My Love*; *Takin' A Holiday* • John Mathiason: *12th Street* • Carl Lee Perkins: *Blue Suede Shoes* • Alex Carvin: *Back To School*

3. Ödipus Ratlos (*Oedipus Wrecks*)

Regie: Woody Allen **Drehbuch:** Woody Allen **Produktion:** Robert Greenhut **Kamera:** Sven Nykvist **Schnitt:** Susan E. Morse **Kostüme:** Jeffrey Kurland **Musik:** s. Musiktitel
Darsteller: Woody Allen (*Sheldon Mills*); Mia Farrow (*Lisa*); Julie Kavner (*Treva*); Mae Questel (*Sheldons Mutter*); Marvin Chatinover (*Psychiater*); Molly Regan (*Sheldons Sekretärin*); Ira Wheeler (*Mr. Bates*); Joan Bud (*Vorstandsmitglied*); Jessie Keosian (*Tante Ceil*); Michael Rizzo (*Kellner*); George Schindler (*Shandu, der Magier*); Bridgit Ryan (*Rita*); Larry David (*Theaterdirektor*); Paul Herman (*Detective Flynn*); Herschel Rosen (*Verkäufer*); Lola André/Martin Rosenblatt/Helen Hanft/Annie-Joe Edwards/Ernst Muller/Adele French/Selma Hirsch/Briz/Lou Ruggiero/Elana Cooper (*Mitbürger*); Andrew MacMillan (*Nachrichtensprecher*); Jodi Long/Nancy Giles (*TV-Interviewerinnen*); Mayor Edward I. Koch (*er selbst*); Mike Starr/Richard Grund (*Bauarbeiter*) Ungenannt[1]: Kirsten Dunst/Dylan O'Sullivan Farrow (*Lisas Töchter*)

Handlung: Der erfolgreiche Anwalt Sheldon Mills leidet auch mit fünfzig Jahren noch unter seiner dominanten Mutter. Bei einer Vorstellung des Magiers Shandu verschwindet sie spurlos…

Musiktitel: Frankie Carle: *I Want A Girl* • Howard Johnson/Theodore Morse: *Mother* • Louis Prima: *Sing, Sing, Sing* • Albert W. Ketèlbey: *In A Persian Market* • Sammy Fain/Irving Kahal: *I'll Be Seeing You* • Jack Palmer/Spencer Williams: *I've Found A New Baby* • Jerome Kern/Oscar Hammerstein II: *All The Things You Are* • Ralph Rainger/Leo Robin: *June In January* • Giacomo Puccini: *Nessun dorma*, aus der Oper *Turandot*

1989

Verbrechen Und Andere Kleinigkeiten
(*Crimes And Misdemeanors*)
USA, ca. 100 Minuten

Regie: Woody Allen **Drehbuch:** Woody Allen **Produktion:** Robert Greenhut **Kamera:** Sven Nykvist **Schnitt:** Susan E. Morse **Kostüme:** Jeffrey Kurland **Musik:** s. Musiktitel **Darsteller:** Caroline Aaron (*Barbara*); Alan Alda (*Lester*); Woody Allen (*Cliff Stern*); Claire Bloom (*Miriam Rosenthal*); Mia Farrow (*Halley Reed*); Joanna Gleason (*Wendy Stern*); Anjelica Huston (*Dolores Paley*); Martin Landau (*Judah Rosenthal*); Jenny Nichols (*Jenny*); Jerry Orbach (*Jack Rosenthal*); Sam Waterston (*Ben*); Bill Bernstein (*Festredner*); Stephanie Roth Haberle (*Sharon Rosenthal*); Gregg Edelman (*Chris*); George Manos (*Fotograf*); Zina Jasper (*Carol*); Dolores Sutton (*Judahs Sekretärin*); Joel S. Fogel/Donna Castellano/Thomas P. Crow (*TV-Produzenten*); Martin S. Bergmann (*Prof. Louis Levy*); Kenny Vance (*Murray*); Jerry Orbach (*Jack Rosenthal*); Jerry Zaks (*Mann auf dem Campus*); Barry Finkel/Steve Maidment (*Fernseh-Autoren*); Nadia Sanford (*Alva*); Chester Malinowski (*Killer*); Stanley Reichman (*Chris' Vater*); Rebecca Schull (*Chris' Mutter*); David S. Howard (*Sol Rosenthal*); Garrett Simowitz (*junger Judah*); Frances Conroy (*Hausbesitzerin*); Anna Berger (*Tante May*); Sol Frieder/Justin Zaremby/Marvin Terban/Hy Anzell/Sylvia Kauders (*Sedergäste*); Victor Argo (*Detektiv*); Leonore Loveman/Nora Ephron/Sunny Keyser/Merv Bloch/Nancy Arden/Thomas L. Bolster/Myla Pitt/Robin Bartlett (*Hochzeitsgäste*); Grace Zimmerman (*Braut*); Randy Aaron Fink (*Bräutigam*); Rabbi Joel Zion (*Rabbi*); Major Halley Jr./Walter Levinsky/George Masso/Charles Miles/Derek Smith/Warren Vaché (*Jazz Band*); Pete Antell/Anthony Gorruso/Gary Allen Meyers/Lee Musiker/Tony Sotos/Tony Tedesco (*Hochzeitsband*) *Ungenannt[1]:* Daryl Hannah (*Lisa Crosley*); Fred Melamed (*Dekan*); Dylan O'Sullivan Farrow (*kleines Mädchen bei der Hochzeitsfeier*)

Handlung: Zwei ganz unterschiedliche Männer in Konfliktsituationen: Augenarzt Judah Rosenthal wird von seiner Geliebten erpresst und sucht nach einem Ausweg, denn seine Ehe und sein Ansehen stehen auf dem Spiel… Der sympathische, aber glücklose Dokumentarfilmer Cliff Stern muss notgedrungen einen Film über seinen verhassten Schwager Lester drehen, einen ebenso oberflächlichen wie leider auch erfolgreichen Produzenten. Bei den Dreharbeiten verlieben sich beide in dieselbe Frau… Am Ende kommt es zu einem denkwürdigen Zusammentreffen der beiden Protagonisten Judah und Cliff…

Musiktitel: Cole Porter: *Rosalie* • Edward Ward: aus „*Mr. & Mrs. Smith*" • Richard Rodgers/Lorenz Hart: *Dancing On The Ceiling* • Vernon Duke/John LaTouche: *Taking A Chance On Love* • Vincent Youmans/Anne Caldwell: *I Know That You Know* • Johann Sebastian Bach: *Englische Suite Nr. 2 a*-Moll BWV 807 • Hilton Ruiz: *Home Cooking* • Mildred J. Hill/Patty S. Hill: *Happy Birthday To You* • Ben Bernie/Kenneth Casey/Maceo Pinkard: *Sweet Georgia Brown* • Frank Loesser/Jacques Press: *I've Got You* • Irving Berlin: *This Year's Kisses* • Nacio Herb Brown/Arthur Freed: *All I Do Is Dream Of You*, aus „*Singin' In The Rain*" • Franz Schubert: *Streichquartett Nr. 15 G-*Dur op. 161 (D 887), 1. *Allegro Molto Moderato* • Frank Loesser/Jimmy McHugh: *Murder He Says*, aus „*Happy Go Lucky*" • Victor Young/Wayne King/Egbert Van Alstyne/Haven Gillespie: *Beautiful Love* • Vincent Youmans/William Rose/Edward Eliscu: *Great Day* • Gene de Paul: *Star Eyes* • Guy D'Hardelot/Edward Teschemacher: *Because* • Irving Caesar/Joseph Meyer/R. Wolfe Kahn: *Crazy Rhythm* • Noel Coward: *I'll See You Again* • Xavier Cugat/Rafael Angulo/Jack Wiseman: *Cuban Mambo* • Johnny Burke/Jimmy Van Heusen: *Polkadots And Moonbeams* • Sammy Fain/Irving Kahal: *I'll Be Seeing You*

1990

Alice
(*Alice*)
USA, ca. 102 Minuten

Regie: Woody Allen **Drehbuch:** Woody Allen **Produktion:** Robert Greenhut **Kamera:** Carlo Di Palma **Schnitt:** Susan E. Morse **Kostüme:** Jeffrey Kurland **Musik:** s. Musiktitel
Darsteller: Alec Baldwin (*Ed*); Blythe Danner (*Dorothy*); Judy Davis (*Vicki*); Mia Farrow (*Alice Tate*); William Hurt (*Doug Tate*); Keye Luke (*Dr. Yang*); Joe Mantegna (*Joe*); Bernadette Peters (*Muse*); Cybill Shepherd (*Nancy Brill*); Gwen Verdon (*Alice' Mutter*); Caroline Aaron (*Sue*); Bob Balaban (*Sid Moscowitz*); Robin Bartlett (*Nina*); Julie Kavner (*Raumausstatterin*); Patrick O'Neal (*Alice' Vater*); Diane Salinger (*Carol*); David Spielberg (*Ken*); Linda Wallem (*Penny*); June Squibb (*Hilda*); Marceline Hugot (*Monica*); Dylan O'Sullivan Farrow (*Kate*); Matt Williamson (*Dennis*); Billy Taylor (*Trainer*); Holland Taylor (*Helen*); Michael-Vaughn Sullivan (*Friseur*); Gina Gallagher (*Joes Tochter*); Patience Moore (*Lehrerin*); Diana Cheng (*Dr. Yangs Assistentin*); Kim Chan (*Dr. Yangs Patient*); Lynda Bridges (*Verkäuferin*); Anthony Cortino (*Hundefriseur*); Katja Schumann (*Luftakrobatin*); Vanessa Thomas (*Zirkusreiterin*); Kristy Graves (*Alice mit 18 Jahren*); Laurie Nayber (*junge Dorothy*); Rachel Miner (*Alice mit 12 Jahren*); Amy Louise Barrett (*Mrs. Keyes*); Alexi Henry (*Kimberly*); James Toback (*Professor*); Elle Macpherson (*Model*); Ira Wheeler/Lisa Marie (*Gäste beim Büro-Weihnachtsfest*); Alfred Cherry (*Vickis Analytiker*); Peggy Miley (*Dorothys Hausangestellte*); George Manos/Kim Weston-Moran/Peter Tolan/Kenneth Edelson/Marvin Terban/James McDaniel/Roy Attaway (*Gäste bei Dorothys Weihnachtsparty*); Jodi Long/Suzann O'Neill/Don Snell/Robert Polenz (*Park-Avenue-Paare*)

Handlung: Alice Tate führt ein privilegiertes Leben als Ehefrau und Mutter in Manhattan. Trotzdem scheint ihr etwas zu fehlen. Als sie sich in den Musiker Joe verliebt, sucht sie Rat bei einem chinesischen Arzt. Der verändert mit unkonventionellen Methoden ihren Blick auf die Welt…

Musiktitel: Philip Braham/Douglas Furber: *Limehouse Blues* • Dizzy Gillespie/Seymour Simons/Richard A. Whiting: *Breezin' Along With The Breeze* • Jerome Kern/Dorothy Fields: *I Dream Too Much*; *The Way You Look Tonight* • Will Hudson/Irving Mills/Eddie DeLange: *Moonglow* • Matos Rodríguez: *La Cumparsita* • Linda Hudes: *The Courier*; *World Music* • Duke Ellington/Juan Tizol/Irving Mills: *Caravan* • Johnny Mercer/Victor Schertzinger: *I Remember You* • Johnny Burke/Jimmy Van Heusen: *Moonlight Becomes You* • Joseph McCarthy/Harry Tierney: *Alice Blue Gown* • Johann Sebastian Bach: *Violinkonzert a-Moll BWV 1041, 1. Allegro* • Eddie DeLange/Jimmy Van Heusen: *Darn That Dream* • Danny Alguire/Frank Thomas/Ward Kimball: *Southern Comfort* • Kurt Weill/Bertolt Brecht: *Die Moritat Von Mackie Messer*, aus der *Dreigroschenoper* • Neal Hefti: *Flight Of The Foo Birds* • Matt Dennis/Tom Adair: *Will You Still Be Mine* • Weihnachtslieder: *Oh Tannenbaum*; *We Wish You A Merry Christmas*

1991

Schatten Und Nebel
(*Shadows And Fog*)
USA, ca. 82 Minuten s/w

Regie: Woody Allen **Drehbuch:** Woody Allen **Produktion:** Robert Greenhut **Kamera:** Carlo Di Palma **Schnitt:** Susan E. Morse **Kostüme:** Jeffrey Kurland **Musik:** Kurt Weill
Darsteller: Woody Allen (*Kleinman*); John Cusack (*Student Jack*); Mia Farrow (*Irmy*); Lily Tomlin/Jodie Foster/Kathy Bates/Anne Lange (*Prostituierte*); Fred Gwynne/Robert Silver (*Hackers Gefolgsleute*); Julie Kavner (*Alma*); Madonna (*Marie*); John Malkovich (*Clown*); Kenneth Mars (*Illusionist*); Kate Nelligan (*Eve*); Donald Pleasance (*Arzt*); Michael Kirby (*Killer*); David Ogden Stiers (*Hacker*); James Rebhorn/Victor Argo/Daniel Von Bargen (*Bürgerwehr*); Camille Saviola (*Hauswirtin*); Tim Loomis (*Zwerg*); Katy Dierlam (*Dicke Frau*); Dennis Vestunis (*starker Mann*); Andrew Mark Berman/Paul Anthony Stewart/Thomas L. Bolster (*Studenten*); Fred Melamed (*Beobachter der unerwünschten Personen*); Greg Stebner (*Polizeichef*); Peter Appel/John C. Reilly/Brian Smiar/Michael P. Troy/Remak Ramsay/Ron Turek (*Polizisten auf der Wache*); Philip Bosco (*Mr. Paulsen*); Peter McRobbie (*Barmann*); Josef Sommer (*Priester*); Ira Wheeler (*Polizist mit Priester*); Eszter Balint (*Frau mit Baby*); Rebecca Gibson (*Baby*); Kurtwood Smith (*Vogels Gefolgsmann*); Charles Cragin (*Spiro*); Robert Joy (*Sprios Assistent*); W. H. Macy (*Polizist mit Spiro*); Tom Riis Farrell/Ron Weyand (*Bürgerwehr mit Spiro*); Wallace Shawn (*Simon Carr*); Richard Riehle/Max Robinson (*Handlanger*)

Handlung: In einem kleinen Ort in Europa in den 20er Jahren geht ein Mörder um. Die Bürgerwehr macht sich auf die Suche und holt auch den Angestellten Max Kleinman mitten in der Nacht aus dem Bett, damit er sich an der Aktion beteiligt. Kurze Zeit später wird Kleinman selbst zum Verdächtigen…

> Der Film ist ein „*Ausflug in die europäische Filmgeschichte, in eine Welt kafkaesker Nachtmahre […].*"[6]
> „*In seinem […] Film […] ging es dem 1935 geborenen Juden um die Kälte des Holocaust.*"[7]

Musiktitel: Kurt Weill/Bertolt Brecht: *Kanonenlied*, aus der *Dreigroschenoper*; *Prolog*, aus *Die Sieben Todsünden*; *Alabama Song*, aus der Oper *Aufstieg und Fall der Stadt Mahagonny*; *Die Moritat Von Mackie Messer*, aus der *Dreigroschenoper* • Robert Katscher/B. G. DeSylva: *When Day Is Done* • Kurt Schwabach/Austin Egen: *Ja, Ja Die Frau'n Sind Meine Schwache Seite* • Franz Doelle/Fritz Rotter: *Wenn Der Weiße Flieder Wieder Blüht*

---

[6] Hellmuth Karasek: Ein New Yorker in Prag. In: Der Spiegel 10/1992
[7] Alice Schwarzer: Adieu, Woody Allen. In: Emma 10/1992

1991

Ein Ganz Normaler Hochzeitstag
(*Scenes From A Mall*)
USA, ca. 89 Minuten

Regie: Paul Mazursky **Drehbuch**: Roger L. Simon/Paul Mazursky **Produktion:** Paul Mazursky **Kamera:** Fred Murphy **Schnitt:** Stuart Pappé **Kostüme:** Albert Wolsky **Musik**: Marc Shaiman **Darsteller:** Bette Midler (*Deborah*); Woody Allen (*Nick*); Bill Irwin (*Pantomime*); Daren Firestone (*Sam*); Rebecca Nickels (*Jennifer*); Paul Mazursky (*Dr. Hans Clava*); Gregory Moore/Michael Brown/Jonathan Guss/David Frye (*Friseurladen-Quartett*); Joseph Warren/Brian Warren/Darrell Mason (*Rapper: Joe Cool & The Coolers*); Marc Shaiman (*Pianist*); Augustin Bustamante/Leonel Cruz/Telmo Hernandez/Steve Ortiz/Ramon Ponce/Fernando Quinones (*El Mariachi Bustamante*); Joan Delaney (*Interviewerin*); Amanda Bruce (*Interviewgast*); Betsy Mazursky (*Frau am Informationsstand*); Jack Brodsky (*Apotheker*); Glen Alterman (*Museumsshop-Besitzer*); Marilyn Pasekoff (*Frau im Buchladen*); Patrick Farrelly (*Weihnachtsmann*); Hidehiko Takada (*Sushi-Chef*); Tichina Arnold (*Ticketverkäuferin*); Wanakee Legardy (*Verkäuferin im Bekleidungsgeschäft*); Carol Harris (*Kellnerin im Nuvo Navajo*); Vira Colorado/Billy Graham (*Security*); Chun Long Zhang (*Chinesischer Akrobat*); Kamarr (*Zauberer*); Kathy Kamarr (*Assistentin des Zauberers*); Robert Garrett (*Barmann*); Fabio Lanzoni (*attraktiver junger Mann*); Steven Dominic Prestianni/Heather Golden (*Sikh-Pärchen*); José Rafael Arango (*Junge auf dem Bus*); Bobby Caravella (*Mann im Parkhaus*); Laura Baler (*Süßwarenmädchen*); James Duane Polk (*Mann in der Kinoschlange*); Penny Gaston/Minna Rose/Stewart Russell/Joe Viviani (*Apothekenkunden*); Larry Sherman/Shirô Oishi/Ron Barry-Barry (*Männer an Autotelefonen*); Michael Greene/Stuart Pappé (*Motorradfahrer*); Andre Philippe (*Taxifahrer*); Phillip Nozaki/Donnie Kelber (*Kinder im Van*); Rene Victor/Ann Lochart/Pam Hayden (*Stimmen*) *Ungenannt[1]:* Soon-Yi Previn (*Frau in der Schlange*)

Handlung: Anwalt Nick und seine Frau, die Psychologin Deborah, bereiten die Feier zu ihrem 16. Hochzeitstag zunächst in schönster Eintracht vor. Später kommt es in einem Einkaufszentrum jedoch zu heftigen Auseinandersetzungen zwischen den beiden und Deborah möchte die Feier am liebsten absagen…

Musiktitel: Cole Porter: *You Do Something To Me*; *Let's Do It*; *Easy To Love* • Leonard Whitcup/George Douglas: *Give Me Your Kisses* • Joseph E. Warren: *The Christmas Break*; *Wyze Man* • Felix Bernard/Dick Smith: *Winter Wonderland* • Pat Ballard: *Mister Santa* • Johnny Marks: *Rudolph The Red-Nosed Reindeer* • Les Applegate: *Coney Island Baby* • Tomas Mendez: *Cucurrucucu* • Pepe Guizar: *Guadalajara* • Nicandro Castillo: *La Calandria* • Passion Play: *Hurricane* • J. Leach: *Arabian Belly Dance* • Traditionelles Weihnachtslied: „*Deck The Halls*" • Jack Lawrence/Walter Gross: *Tenderly* • Nino Rota: Thema aus dem Soundtrack von "*Amarcord*"; Thema aus dem Soundtrack von „*Juliet Of The Spirits*"

1992

Ehemänner Und Ehefrauen
(*Husbands And Wives*)
USA, ca. 103 Minuten

Regie: Woody Allen **Drehbuch:** Woody Allen **Produktion:** Robert Greenhut **Kamera:** Carlo Di Palma **Schnitt:** Susan E. Morse **Kostüme:** Jeffrey Kurland **Musik** s. Musiktitel **Darsteller:** Woody Allen (*Gabe Roth*); Blythe Danner/Brian McConnachie (*Rains Eltern*); Judy Davis (*Sally*); Mia Farrow (*Judy Roth*); Juliette Lewis (*Rain*); Liam Neeson (*Michael Gates*); Sydney Pollack (*Jack*); Jeffrey Kurland (*Erzähler*); Bruce Jay Friedman (*Peter Styles*); Cristi Conaway (*Shawn Grainger*); Timothy Jerome (*Paul*); Rebecca Glenn (*Gail*); Galaxy Craze (*Harriet*); Lysette Anthony (*Sam*); Benno Schmidt (*Judys Ex-Ehemann*); Nick Metropolis (*Wissenschaftler im Fernsehen*); John Doumanian/Gordon Rigsby (*Hampton-Partygäste*); Ilene Blackman (*Empfangsdame*); Ron Rifkin (*Rains Analytiker*); Ron August/John Bucher (*Rains Ex-Liebhaber*); Matthew Flint (*Rains Freund*); Jerry Zaks/Caroline Aaron/Jack Richardson/Nora Ephron/Ira Wheeler (*Dinnerparty-Gäste*); Kenneth Edelson/Michelle Turley/Victor Truro/Kenny Vance/Lisa Gustin/Anthony Nocerino (*Gabes Romanfiguren*); Philip Levy (*Taxi-Disponent*); Connie Picard/Steven Randazzo/Tony Turco/Adelaide Mestre (*Familie Banducci*); Jessica Frankston/Merv Bloch (*Geburtstagsparty-Gäste*) *Ungenannt*[1]: Fred Melamed (*Mel*)

Handlung: Als das Ehepaar Gabe und Judy Roth (Professor für Literatur und Redakteurin eines Kunstmagazins) von der Trennung ihrer Freunde Sally und Jack erfährt, sind beide schockiert und fangen an, ihre eigene Beziehung zu hinterfragen… An den letzten Drehtagen des Films kommt es zum Bruch zwischen Woody Allen und seiner langjährigen Lebensgefährtin Mia Farrow.

Musiktitel: Cole Porter: *What Is This Thing Called Love?* • Wes Montgomery: *West Coast Blues* • Gustav Mahler: *Sinfonie Nr. 9 D-Dur, 1. Andante comodo* • Lew Brown/Sammy Fain: *That Old Feeling* • Irving Berlin: *Top Hat, White Tie And Tails* • Walter Donaldson/Gus Kahn: *Makin' Whoopee* • Jerome Kern/Oscar Hammerstein II: *The Song Is You*

1993

Manhattan Murder Mystery
(*Manhattan Murder Mystery*)
USA, ca. 103 Minuten

Regie: Woody Allen **Drehbuch:** Woody Allen/Marshall Brickman **Produktion:** Robert Greenhut **Kamera:** Carlo Di Palma **Schnitt:** Susan E. Morse **Kostüme:** Jeffrey Kurland **Musik:** s. Musiktitel **Darsteller:** Alan Alda (*Ted*); Woody Allen (*Larry Lipton*); Anjelica Huston (*Marcia Fox*); Diane Keaton (*Carol Lipton*); Jerry Adler (*Paul House*); Joy Behar (*Marilyn*); Ron Rifkin (*Sy*); Lynn Cohen (*Lillian House*); William Addy (*Jack*); John Doumanian/Sylvia Kauders (*Nachbarn*); Ira Wheeler (*Notarzt*); Mélanie Norris (*Helen Moss*); Marge Redmond (*Mrs. Dalton*); Zach Braff (*Nick Lipton*); George Manos/Linda Taylor (*Club-21-Angestellte*); Aida Turturro (*Hotelangestellte*); John Costelloe/Frank Pellegrino/Philip Levy/Wendell Pierce/Steven Randazzo (*Polizisten*); Yanni Sfinias (*Nachtportier*); Gloria Irizarry (*Zimmermädchen*); Ruth Last (*Lillians Schwester*); Suzanne Raffaelli (*Theaterbesucherin*)

Handlung: Ein verdächtiger Todesfall in der Nachbarwohnung ist der willkommene Anlass für Verlegersgattin Carol aus ihrer Alltagsroutine auszubrechen. Und so beginnt sie auf eigene Faust Nachforschungen anzustellen. Ehemann Larry zeigt zunächst kein Interesse, bis sich die Verdachtsmomente gegen den Nachbarn erhärten. Unterstützt wird das Paar vom gemeinsamen Freund Ted, der für Larrys Geschmack inzwischen schon etwas zu vertraut mit Carol zu sein scheint… Woody Allen zitiert im Film die berühmte „Spiegelkabinett-Szene" aus Orson Wells' „The Lady From Shanghai".

Musiktitel: Cole Porter: *I Happen To Like New York* • Lew Brown/B. G. DeSylva/Ray Henderson: *The Best Things In Life Are Free* • Miklós Rózsa: *The Hallway* • Richard Wagner: aus der Oper *Der Fliegende Holländer* • Paul Desmond: *Take Five* • Jimmy McHugh/Dorothy Fields: *I'm In The Mood For Love* • Bob Haggart/Ray Bauduc/Gil Rodin/Bob Crosby: *The Big Noise From Winnetka* • Johnny Green/Edward Heyman: *Out Of Nowhere* • Lorenz Hart/Richard Rodgers: *Have You Met Miss Jones* • Frank Loesser: *Ouvertüre* zu *Guys And Dolls* • Louis Prima: *Sing, Sing, Sing* • Errol Garner: *Misty*

1994

Bullets Over Broadway
(*Bullets Over Broadway*)
USA, ca. 95 Minuten

Regie: Woody Allen **Drehbuch:** Woody Allen/Douglas McGrath **Produktion:** Robert Greenhut **Kamera:** Carlo Di Palma **Schnitt:** Susan E. Morse **Kostüme:** Jeffrey Kurland **Musik:** Dick Hyman **Darsteller:** Jim Broadbent (*Warner Purcell*); John Cusack (*David Shayne*); Harvey Fierstein (*Sid Loomis*); Chazz Palminteri (*Cheech*); Mary-Louise Parker (*Ellen*); Rob Reiner (*Sheldon Flender*); Jennifer Tilly (*Olive Neal*); Tracey Ullman (*Eden Brent*); Joe Viterelli (*Nick Valenti*); Jack Warden (*Julian Marx*); Dianne Wiest (*Helen Sinclair*); Tony Sirico (*Rocco*); Victor Colicchio/Lou Eppolito/Gene Canfield/Peter Castellotti/Tony Conforti/John DiBenedetto/Johnny Ventimiglia (*Gangster am Hafen*); Lisa Arturo/Rachel Black/Alison Cramer/Kelly Groninger/Jennifer Lamberts/Carol Lee Meadows/Jo Telford/Meghan Strange/Leigh Torlage/Debra Wiseman (*Three Deuces Tanzgruppe*); Paul Herman (*Oberkellner*); James Reno (*Sal*); Stacey Nelkin (*Rita*); Margaret Sophie Stein (*Lili*); Charles Cragin (*Rifkin*); Gerald E. Dolezar (*Café-Kellner*); Nina Sonya Peterson (*Josette*); Shannah Laumeister/Fran McGee (*Schießerei-Opfer vor dem Kino*); Annie-Joe Edwards (*Venus*); Brian McConnachie (*Mitch Sabine*); Edie Falco (*Lorna*); Kernan Bell (*Kellner in der Flüsterkneipe*); Hope W. Sacharoff (*Hilda Marx*); Debi Mazar (*Vi*); Nick Iacovino/Frank Aquilino (*Gangster*); Sam Ardeshir/Molly Regan (*Helens Partygäste*); Phil Stein (*Bühnenarbeiter*); John Doumanian/Dayle Haddon (*Gratulanten hinter den Kulissen*); Tony Darrow (*Aldo*); Howard Erskine/Benay Venuta/Ken Roberts (*Gratulanten vor dem Theater*); Jennifer Van Dyck (*Zweitbesetzung für Olive*); Peter McRobbie (*Mann beim Theater*) **Ungenannt**[1]: Jeff Mazzola (*Kino-Killer*)

Handlung: New York in den 20er Jahren: Theaterautor David Shayne möchte sein neues Stück am Broadway aufführen. Leider braucht er dafür finanzielle Unterstützung von Mafioso Nick Valenti. Nicks Bedingung: Seine Geliebte, das Revuegirl Olive, darf die Hauptrolle spielen. Im Laufe der Proben greift dann auch noch Olives Leibwächter Cheech verstärkt in die Produktion ein…

Musiktitel: Gus Kahn/Ernie Erdman/Dan Russo: *Toot, Toot, Tootsie* • Sidney Clare/Con Conrad: *Ma, He's Making Eyes At Me* • Billy Rose/Con Conrad: *You've Got To See Mamma Ev'ry Night* • Jerome Kern/Oscar Hammerstein II: *Make Believe* • Andy Razaf/Harry Brooks/Fats Waller: *That Jungle Jamboree* • Con Conrad/Sam M. Lewis/J. Russel Robinson/Joe Young: *Singin' The Blues Till My Daddy Comes Home* • Hoagy Carmichael/Sidney Arodin: *Lazy River* • Raymond Hubbell/John Golden: *Poor Butterfly* • Cole Porter: *Let's Misbehave* • Richard Rodgers/Lorenz Hart: *You Took Advantage Of Me*; *Thou Swell* • Harry Woods: *When The Red, Red Robin Comes Bob Bob Bobbin' Along* • Irving Caesar/Joseph Meyer/Roger Wolfe Kahn: *Crazy Rhythm* • D.J. LaRocca/Larry Shields: *At The Jazz Band Ball* • Harry Warren/Mort Dixon: *Nagasaki* • George Gershwin/Ira Gershwin: *That Certain Feeling* • Jerome Kern/Otto Harbach/Oscar Hammerstein II: *Who*

1995

Geliebte Aphrodite
(*Mighty Aphrodite*)
USA, ca. 95 Minuten

Regie: Woody Allen **Drehbuch:** Woody Allen **Produktion:** Robert Greenhut **Kamera:** Carlo Di Palma **Schnitt:** Susan E. Morse **Kostüme:** Jeffrey Kurland **Musik:** Dick Hyman
Darsteller: F. Murray Abraham (*Chorleiter*); Woody Allen (*Lenny*); Claire Bloom (*Amandas Mutter*); Helena Bonham Carter (*Amanda*); Olympia Dukakis (*Iocaste*); Michael Rapaport (*Kevin*); Mira Sorvino (*Linda Ash*); David Ogden Stiers (*Laius*); Jack Warden (*Tiresias*); Peter Weller (*Jerry Bender*); Kathleen Doyle (*Frau des Ex-Vermieters*); Danielle Ferland (*Cassandra*); Jimmy McQuaid (*Max*); Peter McRobbie (*Lindas Ex-Vermieter*); Dan Moran (*Ricky, der Zuhälter*); Dan Mullane (*Bote*); Steven Randazzo (*Bud*); J. Smith Cameron (*Buds Frau*); Pamela Blair/René Ceballos/Elie Chaib/George De La Pena/Joanne DiMauro/Denise Faye/Marianne Filali/Angelo Fraboni/Scott Fowler/Seth Gertsacov/Patti Karr/Fred Mann III/John Mineo/Christopher Nelson/Valda Setterfield/Sven Toorvald (*Griechischer Chor*); Jeffrey Kurland (*Ödipus*); Tucker Robin (*Max als Kind*); Donald Symington (*Amandas Vater*); Nolan Tuffy (*zweijähriger Max*); Yvette Hawkins (*Schuldirektorin*); Karin Haidorfer/Gary Alper (*Park Avenue Paar*); Rosemary Murphy (*Adoptionsvermittlerin*); Jennifer Greenhut (*Lennys Sekretärin*); Sondra James (*Vermittlung*); Paul Giamatti (*Statistengewerkschaftsrecherche*); William Addy (*Superintendent*); Kenneth Edelson (*Ken*); Thomas Durkin (*Ansager beim Pferderennen*); Paul Herman (*Rickys Freund*); Tony Sirico/Tony Darrow/Ray Garvey (*Boxtrainer*); Kent Blocher (*Stimme von Zeus*); Joseph P. Coleman/Georgette Pasare (*Pornofilmstars*); Al Cerullo (*echter Hubschrauberpilot*); Bray Poor (*Film-Hubschrauberpilot*); David H. Kramer/Dann Fink/Sondra James/Karen Longwell/Dominic Marcus/Craig Sechler/Bill Timoney/Lisa Vidal/Bruce Winant (*Chorstimmen*) **Ungenannt**[1]: Julie Halston (*Gast*)

Handlung: Sportreporter Lenny ist erst gar nicht begeistert, als seine Frau Amanda vorschlägt, ein Kind zu adoptieren. Doch Amanda setzt sich durch und sofort ist Lenny ganz vernarrt in den kleinen Jungen. So sehr, dass er unbedingt die leibliche Mutter des Kindes kennenlernen möchte. Als er sich gegen alle Vorschriften tatsächlich ihren Namen und die Adresse verschafft, nimmt das Schicksal seinen so nicht vorbestimmten Lauf… Wie im antiken griechischen Theater werden die Ereignisse von einem Chor begleitet und kommentiert.

Musiktitel: Vasilis Tsitsanis: *Neo Minore* • Richard Rodgers/Lorenz Hart: *Manhattan* • Will Jason/Val Burton: *Penthouse Serenade* • Jack Palmer/Spencer Williams: *I've Found A New Baby* • Paul Desmond: *Take Five* • Billy Page: *The ‚In' Crowd* • Neal Hefti: *Li'l Darlin'* • Fred E. Ahlert/Roy Turk: *Walkin' My Baby Back Home* • Stavros Xarhakos: *Horos Tou Sakena* • Richard Coburn/Vincent Rose/John Schonberger: *Whispering* • Cole Porter: *You Do Something To Me* • Ray Noble: *I Hadn't Anyone Till You* • Aaron Einar Swan: *When Your Lover Has Gone* • Bobby Gosh: *FAO Schwarz Clock Tower Song* • Mark Fisher/Joe Goodwin/Larry Shay: *When You're Smiling*

1996

Alle Sagen: I Love You
(*Everyone Says I Love You*)
USA, ca. 97 Minuten

Regie: Woody Allen **Drehbuch:** Woody Allen **Produktion:** Robert Greenhut **Kamera:** Carlo Di Palma **Schnitt:** Susan E. Morse **Kostüme:** Jeffrey Kurland **Musik:** Dick Hyman **Darsteller:** Woody Allen (*Joe Berlin*); Alan Alda (*Bob Dandridge*); Drew Barrymore (*Skylar Dandridge*); Lukas Haas (*Scott*); Goldie Hawn (*Steffi Dandridge*); Gaby Hoffmann (*Lane*); Natasha Lyonne (*DJ*); Edward Norton (*Holden Spence*); Natalie Portman (*Laura Dandridge*); Julia Roberts (*Von*); Tim Roth (*Charles Ferry*); David Ogden Stiers (*Arnold Spence*); Scotty Bloch (*Lynn Spence*); Patrick Cranshaw (*Großvater*); Billy Crudup (*Ken*); Trude Klein (*Frieda*); Robert Knepper (*Greg*); Itzhak Perlman (*er selbst*); Navah Perlman (*Pianist*); Barbara Hollander (*Claire*); John Griffin (*Jeffrey Vandermost*); Waltrudis Buck (*Psychiaterin*); Edward Hibbert (*Harry-Winston-Verkäufer*); Paolo Seganti (*DJ's Venedig-Date*); Andrea Piedimonte (*Alberto*); Ed Hodson (*Scotts Arzt*); Michel Moinot (*Bobs Arzt*); Diva Gray/Ami Almendral/Madeline Balmaceda (*Nannies*); Vivian Cherry (*Krankenschwester*); Tommie Baxter (*Alte Frau*); Jeff Derocker (*Obdachloser*); Cherylyn Jones/Tina Paul/Vikki Schnurr (*Models*); Kevin Hagan (*Türsteher*); Isiah Whitlock (*Polizist*); Kevin Bogue/Colleen Dunn/Pamela Everett/Susan Misner/Gregory Mitchell/Dana Moore/Troy Myers/Joe Orrach/Michael O'Steeen/Tina Paul/Krissy Richmond (*Harry-Winston-Tänzer*); Luis Martin Perez (*Harry-Winston-Tänzer/Krankenhaus-Tänzer/Geist-Tänzer/Groucho-Party-Tänzer*); Frederick Rolf (*Le-Cirque-Kellner*); Timothy Jerome (*Röntgenarzt*); Daisy Prince/Linda Maurel-Sithole (*Krankenschwestern*); Arlene Martin Martell/Helen Miles (*Krankenschwestern/Helen-Miles-Singers*); René Ceballos/Ruth Gottschall/Colton Green/Lisa LeGuillou/Joe Locarro/Monica McSwain/Jill Nicklaus/Andrew Pacho/John Selya/Myra Lucretia Taylor/Jo Telford (*Krankenhaus-Tänzer*); Robert Khakh (*Taxifahrer*); Gerry Burkhardt/Eileen Casey/Shelley Frankel/Fred Mann III/Kathy Sanson/Valda Setterfield/Frank Pietri (*Geist-Tänzer*); Robert Walker/Devalle Hayes/Damon McCloud (*Rapper*); Tony Sirico/Ray Garvey (*entlaufende Sträflinge*); Tommy John/Lindsy Canuel/Richard Cummings/Kristen Pettet/Patrick Lavery/Christy Romano/Jonathan Giordano/Gabriel Millman (*Trick-or-Treat-Kinder*); Don Correia/Sean Grant/Roland Hayes/Darren Lee/Delphine T. Mantz/Joanne McHugh/John Mineo/Cynthia Onrubia/Willie Rosario/Jerome Vivona/Nancy Ticotin (*Groucho-Party-Tänzer*); Emily Bindinger/Cindy Cobitt/Al Dana/Kevin DeSimone/Paul Evans/Chrissy Faith/Jeff Lyons/Michael Mark/Arlene Martin Martell/Helen Miles/Jenna Miles/Robert Ragaini/Lenny Roberts/Annette Sanders/Terry Textor/Vaneese Thomas/Ashley H. Wilkinson (*Helen Miles Singers*) Ungenannt[1]: Olivia Hayman (*Singstimme von Skylar*)

Handlung: Der Musikfilm dreht sich um das komplizierte Liebesleben verschiedener Mitglieder einer wohlhabenden New Yorker Familie: DJ's Eltern sind geschieden. Mutter Steffie ist inzwischen mit Bob verheiratet. DJ's Vater, der Schriftsteller Joe Berlin, immer noch erfolglos bei der Suche nach einer neuen Frau, zieht seine Ex-Frau und deren Mann gerne in Liebesdingen zu Rate. DJ's Halbschwester muss sich zwischen zwei Männern entscheiden. Als DJ mit ihrem Vater nach Venedig reist, verliebt Joe sich in die schöne Kunsthistorikerin Von. Unglücklicherweise ist Von verheiratet, und außerdem in psychotherapeutischer Behandlung…

Musiktitel: Raymond Klages/Jesse Greer: *Just You, Just Me* • Bert Kalmar/Harry Ruby: *Everyone Says I Love You*; *Hooray For Captain Spaulding* • Walter Donaldson/Gus Kahn: *My Baby Just Cares For Me*; *Makin' Whoopee* • Ray Henderson/Lew Brown/B. G. DeSylva: *I'm A Dreamer, Aren't We All?* • Gus Kahn/Matt Malneck/Fud Livingston: *I'm Thru With Love* • Martin Kalmanoff/Sam Ward/Jack Val/Jimmy Dale/Rodolfo Fabio: *Just Say I Love Her* • Dick Hyman: *Venetian Scenes; Recurrence* • Sam H. Stept/Sidney D. Mitchell: *All My Life* • Karl Hoschna/Otto Harbach: *Cuddle Up A Little Closer* • Cole Porter: *Looking At You* • Jimmy Campbell/Reg Connelly/Ted Shapiro: *If I Had You* • Herb Magidson/Carl Sigman: *Enjoy Yourself* • Larry Clinton: *Satan Takes A Holiday* • Dick Hyman/Robert Walker/Devalle Hayes/Loris Holland: *No Lover, No Friend* • Clarence Gaskill/Jimmy McHugh: *I Can't Believe That You're In Love With Me* • Harry Woods: *What A Little Moonlight Can Do* • William Jerome/Jean Schwartz: *Chinatown, My Chinatown* • Sam Coslow/Arthur Johnston: *Cocktails For Two* • Leonard McKenzie/Garth Montgomery/William Wirges: *Chiquita Banana* • Richard Rodgers/Lorenz Hart: *Mimi* • Leo Robin/Richard A. Whiting: *Louise* • Irving Kahal/Sammy Fain/Pierre Norman: *You Brought A New Kind Of Love To Me*

1996

Sonny Boys – Zwei Wie Pech Und Schwefel
(*The Sunshine Boys*)
USA, ca. 85 Minuten

Regie: John Erman **Drehbuch:** Neil Simon (nach seinem gleichnamigen Theaterstück) **Produktion:** John Erman **Kamera:** Tony Imi **Schnitt:** John W. Wheeler **Kostüme:** Helen Butler **Musik:** Irwin L. Fisch/Stephen Sondheim **Darsteller:** Woody Allen (*Al Lewis*); Peter Falk (*Willie Clark*); Michael McKean (*Scott Grogan*); Liev Schreiber (*Ricky Gregg*); Edie Falco (*Al's Tochter*); Sarah Jessica Parker (*Nancy*); Tyler Noyes (*Peter*); Olga Merediz (*Sue*); Andy Taylor (*Michael Davison*); José Soto (*1. Spanischer Junge*); Kirk Acevedo (*2. Spanischer Junge*); William Hill (*Hal Jenks*); Herbert Rubens (*Murray*); Merwin Goldsmith (*Harry*); David Lipman (*Jerry*); Ray Anthony Thomas (*Limousinenfahrer*); Peter Appel (*Anson Black*); Jennifer Esposito (*Jeannie*); Jim Bracchitta (*Regieassistent*); Michael Badalucco (*Tontechniker*); Stephen Singer (*Kameramann*); Carlos Rafart (*Rezeptionist*) **Ungenannt**[1]: Whoopi Goldberg (*Krankenschwester*)

Handlung: Um das einst erfolgreiche Komiker-Duo Al Lewis und Willie Clark ist es ruhig geworden. Während sich Al schon lange zurückgezogen hat, sucht Willie mit Hilfe seiner Nichte Nancy verzweifelt nach einem neuen Job. Schließlich lockt das Fernsehen mit einem lukrativen Angebot - sofern die beiden Komiker bereit sind, gemeinsam aufzutreten. Doch schon bald brechen schwelende Konflikte zwischen den Rivalen wieder auf…

Musiktitel: Stephen Sondheim: *Old Friends*

1997

Harry Außer Sich
(*Deconstructing Harry*)
USA, ca. 91 Minuten

Regie: Woody Allen **Drehbuch:** Woody Allen **Produktion:** Jean Doumanian **Kamera:** Carlo Di Palma **Schnitt:** Susan E. Morse **Kostüme:** Suzy Benzinger **Musik:** s. Musiktitel
Darsteller: Caroline Aaron (*Doris*); Woody Allen (*Harry Block*); Kirstie Alley (*Joan*); Bob Balaban (*Richard*); Richard Benjamin (*Ken*); Eric Bogosian (*Burt*); Billy Crystal (*Larry/Teufel*); Judy Davis (*Lucy*); Hazelle Goodman (*Cookie*); Mariel Hemingway (*Beth Kramer*); Amy Irving (*Jane*); Julie Kavner (*Grace*); Eric Lloyd (*Hilly*); Julia Louis-Dreyfus (*Leslie*); Tobey Maguire (*Harvey Stern*); Demi Moore (*Helen*); Elisabeth Shue (*Fay*); Stanley Tucci (*Paul Epstein*); Robin Williams (*Mel*); Hy Anzell (*Max*); Scotty Bloch (*Ms. Paley*); Philip Bosco (*Professor Clark*); Robert Harper (*Harrys Arzt*); Shifra Lerer (*Dolly*); Gene Saks (*Harrys Vater*); Stephanie Roth Haberle (*Janet*); Dan Frazer (*Janets Vater*); Joel Leffert (*Norman*); Lynn Cohen (*Janets Mutter*); Joe Buck (*Yankee Ansager*); Jane Hoffman (*Oma*); Annette Arnold (*Rosalee*); Frederick Rolf (*Harveys Arzt*); Elisabeth Anne Cord (*Rosalees Schwester*); Lortensia Hayes (*Jennifer*); Alicia Meer/Victoria Hale (*Frauen im Schuhladen*); Irving Metzman (*Schuhverkäufer*); Sunny Chae (*Lily Chang*); Ralph Pope (*Tod*); Tony Darrow (*Kameramann*); Jonathan LaPaglia (*1. Kamera-Assistent*); Jeff Mazzola (*2. Kamera-Assistent*); Timothy Jerome (*Regisseur*); Peter Castellotti (*Crew Mitglied*); Judy Bauerlein (*Schauspielerin*); Joseph Reidy (*1. Regieassistent*); Phyllis Burdoe (*Scriptgirl*); Barbara Hollander (*Mels Tochter*); Adam Rose (*Mels Sohn*); David S. Howard (*Mels Arzt*); Amanda Barudin (*Beth Kramers Tochter*); Juliet Gelfman-Randazzo (*Baby Hilly*); Floyd Resnick (*israelischer Patient*); Brian McConnachie (*Dr. Reese*); Peter Jacobson (*Goldberg*); Tracey Lynne Miller (*Goldbergs Freundin*); Jennifer Garner (*Frau im Aufzug*); Irwin Charone (*Bar-Mitzvah-Gastgeber*); John Doumanian/Alexa Aronson/Kenneth Edelson (*Bar Mitzvah Gäste*); Viola Harris (*Elsie*); Si Picker (*Wolf Fishbein*); Howard Spiegel (*Mr. Farber*); Eugene Troobnick (*Prof. Wiggins*); Ray Aranha (*Prof. Aranha*); Paul Giamatti (*Prof. Abbot*); Marvin Chatinover (*Prof. Cole*); Daniel Wolf (*Prof. Wolf*); Waltrudis Buck (*Dekanin der Adair Universität*); Arden Myrin (*Studentin Mary*); Daisy Prince (*Fahrstuhl-Stimme*); Peter McRobbie (*Verdammter*); Dan Moran (*Teufel*); Ray Garvey (*Polizist auf dem Campus*); Linda Perri (*Polizistin auf dem Campus*); Tony Sirico (*Polizist im Gefängnis*); Jerry Bruno/Ray Cohen/Michael Manishor/Dave Stettner/Sid Jewkowsky/Bobby Shankin (*Stebbins Hall Band*) **Ungenannt**[1]: Chris Bauer (*Rolle nicht benannt*)

Handlung: Schriftsteller Harry ist zu neurotisch, um im Leben klarzukommen, er funktioniert nur in der Kunst…, und so vermischen sich für ihn bisweilen Realität und Fiktion. Das Ergebnis sind drei gescheiterte Ehen und andere Beziehungskatastrophen. Als ihn auch noch eine Schreibblockade ereilt, gerät Harrys Leben ganz aus den Fugen…

Musiktitel: Wardell Grey/Annie Ross: *Twisted* • Johnny Green/Edward Heyman: *Out Of Nowhere* • Antonio Carlos Jobim/Norman Gimbel/Vinicius de Moraes: *The Girl From Ipanema* • Neil Moret/Richard A. Whiting: *She's Funny That Way* • Glenn Dickson: *Waiting* • Jerome Kern/Oscar Hammerstein II: *All The Things You Are* • Modest Mussorgski: *Eine Nacht Auf Dem Kahlen Berg* • Jerome Kern/Dorothy Fields: *The Way You Look Tonight* • Harry Woods: *When The Red, Red Robin Comes Bob Bob Bobbin' Along* • Cole Porter: *Rosalie* • Irving Fields/Albert Gamse/John A. Camacho: *Miami Beach Rumba* • Julius Grossmann/Issichar Miron/Mitchell Parish: *Tzena Tzena Tzena* • Louis Prima: *Sing, Sing, Sing* • Andy Razaf/Leon Berry: *Christopher Columbus* • Richard Rodgers/Lorenz Hart: *I Could Write A Book* • Wilbur Schwandt/Fabian Andre/Gus Kahn: *Dream A Little Dream Of Me*

1998

Antz
(*Antz*)
USA, ca. 83 Minuten computeranimierter Trickfilm

Regie: Eric Darnell/Tim Johnson **Drehbuch:** Todd Alcott/Chris Weitz/Paul Weitz **Produktion:** Brad Lewis/Aron Warner/Patty Wooton **Schnitt:** Stan Webb **Musik:** Harry Gregson-Williams/John Powell **Sprecher (englisch/deutsch):** Woody Allen/Wolfgang Draeger (*Z*); Dan Aykroyd/Norbert Gescher (*Chip*); Anne Bancroft/Inken Sommer (*Königin*); Jane Curtin/Evelyn Gressmann (*Muffy*); Danny Glover/Jürgen Kluckert (*Barbatus*); Gene Hackman/Klaus Sonnenschein (*Mandible*); Jennifer Lopez/Carola Ewert (*Azteca*); John Mahoney/Helmut Krauss (*betrunkener Scout*); Grant Shaud/Gerald Schaale (*Vorarbeiter*); Sylvester Stallone/Thomas Danneberg (*Weaver*); Sharon Stone/Martina Treger (*Bala*); Christopher Walken/Lutz Riedel (*Cutter*); Paul Mazursky/Lothar Blumhagen (*Psychologe*)

Handlung: Die neurotische Arbeiterameise Z lebt in einem Hügel im Central Park. Beim Psychiater auf der Couch klagt Z über sein Leben als „einer unter Millionen". Und dann verliebt er sich ausgerechnet in die unerreichbare Prinzessin Bala… Antz war einer der ersten vollständig am Computer hergestellten Trickfilme.

Musiktitel: John Lennon: *Give Peace A Chance* • Pete Seeger/Julian Orbon/José Fernández Díaz/José Martí: *Guantanamera* • Alan Jay Lerner/Frederick Loewe: *Almost Like Being In Love* • Johnny Nash: *I Can See Clearly Now* • Sammy Cahn/Jimmy Van Heusen: *High Hopes* • Louis Lambert: *When Johnny Comes Marching Home Again*

1998

Celebrity – Schön, Reich Und Berühmt
(*Celebrity*)
USA, ca. 113 Minuten s/w

Regie: Woody Allen **Drehbuch:** Woody Allen **Produktion:** Jean Doumanian **Kamera:** Sven Nykvist **Schnitt:** Susan E. Morse **Kostüme:** Suzy Benzinger **Musik**: s. Musiktitel **Darsteller:** Hank Azaria (*David*); Kenneth Branagh (*Lee Simon*); Judy Davis (*Robin Simon*); Leonardo DiCaprio (*Brandon Darrow*); Melanie Griffith (*Nicole Oliver*); Famke Janssen (*Bonnie*); Michael Lerner (*Dr. Lupus*); Joe Mantegna (*Tony Gardella*); Bebe Neuwirth (*Nina, die Prostituierte*); Winona Ryder (*Nola*); Charlize Theron (*Supermodel*); Dylan Baker (*Priester im katholischen Retreat*); Kate Burton (*Robins Freundin Cheryl*); Patti D'Arbanville (*Iris*); Karen Duffy (*TV-Journalistin bei der Premiere*); Ned Eisenberg/Richard Mawe/Ted Neustadt/Bruce Jay Friedman/Erica Jong/Clebert Ford (*Gäste bei Elaines Bücher-Party*); Monique Fowler (*Robins Freundin Jan*); Andre Gregory (*John Papadakis*); Allison Janney (*Evelyn Issacs*); Debra Messing (*TV-Journalistin in Lupus' Praxis*); Isaac Mizrahi (*Bruce Bishop*); Gretchen Mol (*Vicky*); Greg Mottola (*Regisseur*); Larry Pine (*Philip Datloff*); Steven Randazzo/John Costelloe (*Polizisten im Hotel*); Adrian Grenier/Sam Rockwell/John Doumanian (*Darrows Entourage*); Aida Turturro (*Olga, Wahrsagerin*); Celia Weston (*Dee Bartholomew*); Jeffrey Wright (*Off-Off Broadway Theaterdirektor*); Jeff Mazzola (*Regieassistent*); Dick Mingalone (*Kameraassistent*); Vladimir Bibic (*Kameramann*); Francisco Quidjada (*Erno Delucca*); Aleksa Palladino (*Produktionsassistentin*); Dan Moran (*Arbeiter am Presslufthammer*); Peter Castellotti (*Tonmeister*); A. Lee Morris (*2. Kameraassistent*); Douglas McGrath (*Bill Gaines*); Maurice Sonnenberg (*Dalton Freed*); Craig Ulmschneider (*Produktionsassistent Daniel*); Mina Bern (*ältere Hausbesitzerin*); Janet Marlow (*Singende Nonne*); Tommie Baxter (*2. Nonne*); Kathleen Doyle/Arthur Berwick/Jodi Long (*Pater Gladdens Fans*); John Carter (*Pater Gladden*); Marylouise Burke/Peter Boyden/Peter McRobbie/Maureen McNamara (*Pater Gladdens Fans auf der Veranda*); Mary Catherine Wright (*Pious Diner*); J.K. Simmons (*Devotionalienverkäufer*); Melinda Eng (*Modedesignerin*); Alma Cuervo/Eve Salvail (*Bewunderer von Bruce Bishops*); Polly Adams/Brian McConnachie (*Trainingsvideo-Fans*); Irina Pantaeva/Mark Vanderloo/Frederique van der Wal (*Freunde des Supermodels*); Anthony Mason (*er selbst*); Daisy Prince (*Krankenschwester im Wartezimmer*); Tina Sloan/Dayle Haddon/Bill Gerber (*Patienten im Wartezimmer*); Julie Halston (*Patientin mit Doppelkinn*); Renée Lippin (*2. Patientin im Untersuchungszimmer*); Reuben Jackson (*Kameramann in Lupus' Büro*); Carmen Dell Orefice (*Pinky Virdon*); Skip Rose/Alicia Meer (*Paar am Strand*); Glenwood High Alumni*: Becky Ann Baker (*Doris**); Michael Kell (*Nat**); Steve Mellor (*Eddie**); Gerry Becker (*Jay Tepper**); Robert Cuccioli (*Monroe Gordon**); Ileen Getz (*Ansagerin beim Glenwood-High-Treffen*); Surinder Khosla (*V.J. Rajnipal*); Frederick Rolf (*Buchkritiker*); David Margulies (*Anwalt Adelman*); Ramsey Faragallah (*TV-Programmdirektor*); William Addy/Patrick McCarthy (*Mitglieder des Ku Klux Klan*); Bernard Addison (*Pfarrer Polynice*); Mary Schmidtberger/Sarah Buff (*TV-Produktionsassistentinnen*); Heather Marni (*fettleibige Teenager-Akrobatin*); Bruno Gioiello/Sean Daloise/Matthew Sweeney (*Skinheads*); Kyle Kulish (*Erfolgreicher Übergewichtiger*); Tony Sirico (*Lou DeMarco*); Kenneth Edelson (*Rabbi Kaufman*); Sam Gray (*Tonys Vater*); Marilyn Raphael (*Tonys Mutter*); Antonette Schwartzberg (*Tonys Großmutter*); Frank Pellegrino (*Frankie*); Gabriel Millman (*Ricky*); Adam Sietz (*Vince*); Michael Crecco/Neal Arluck/Timothy Jerome/Joseph Tudisco (*Hotelangestellte*); Jim Moody/Robert Torres (*Sicherheitsleute*); Mary Joe Buttafuoco (*sie selbst*); Joey Buttafuoco (*er selbst*); Lorri Bagley (*Tschechow-Stil-Autorin*); Ralph Pope (*Agent des Komikers*); Rick Mowat (*Komiker*); Tony Darrow/Victor Colicchio/Robert Cividanes (*Sicherheitsleute im Loft*); Donegal Fitzgerald (*Sicherheitsmann auf der Straße*); Leslie Shenkel („*Manhattan Moods" Direktionsassistent*); Donna Hanover („*Manhattan Moods" Anchor Woman*); Howard Erskine (*Senator Paley*); Donald Trump (*er selbst*); Wood Harris (*Al Swayze*); Ray Cohen (*Pianist bei der Hochzeit*); Angel Caban

(*Limousinenfahrer*); Ingrid Rogers (*Off-Off Broadway Schauspielerin*); Brian McCormack (*Phil*); Gigi Williams (*Fan von Robin Simon*); Michael Moon/Peter Dark/Murphy Occhino/Randy Jordan (*Michael Moon Band*); Richard Iacona/Tom Kirchmer/Stanley Persky/Tony Tedesco/Mike Ponella/Ron Affif (*High School Reunion Band*)

Handlung: Der erfolglose Schriftsteller Lee Simon versucht sich neuerdings als Starreporter und mischt sich dafür unter die Prominenz. Dort bekommt er es unter anderem mit dem egozentrischen Schauspieler Brandon zu tun. Aber auch seine Ex-Frau Robin wird ins Showbusiness eingeführt, mit überraschenden Folgen… Nebenbei führt Woody Allen in verschiedenen Episoden unterschiedlichste Spielarten des Berühmtseins vor. Bemerkenswert: Der Film zeigt die scheinbar so schillernde Welt der Reichen und Schönen in Schwarz-Weiß.

Musiktitel: Dana Suesse/Edward Heyman: *You Oughta Be In Pictures* • Ludwig van Beethoven: *Sinfonie Nr. 5 (Schicksals-Sinfonie)* c-Moll op. 67 • Johnny Mercer/Victor Schertzinger: *Tangerine* • Janet Marlow: *Kumbaya* • Michael Franano: *Chanel No. 5* • Harold Adamson/Walter Donaldson: *Did I Remember* • Fermo Marchetti/Dick Manning: *Fascination* • Bob Weir/Jerry Garcia/Phil Lesh: *Truckin'* • Mitch Leigh/Joe Darion: *The Impossible Dream* • Don McLean: *American Pie* • Eddy R. Davis: *All Hail to You, Glenwood High* • George Gershwin/Ira Gershwin: *I Got Rhythm*; *Soon* • Lew Brown/Sammy Fain: *That Old Feeling* • Matt Dennis/Tom Adair: *Will You Still Be Mine* • George Shearing/George David Weiss: *Lullaby of Birdland* • Frank Loesser: *On A Slow Boat To China* • Sam Coslow/Arthur Johnston: *Cocktails for Two* • Richard Wagner: *Hochzeitsmarsch*, aus der Oper *Lohengrien* • J. Fred Coots/Sam M. Lewis: *For All We Know*

1999

Sweet And Lowdown
(*Sweet And Lowdown*)
USA, ca. 91 Minuten

Regie: Woody Allen **Drehbuch:** Woody Allen **Produktion:** Jean Doumanian **Kamera:** Fei Zhao **Schnitt:** Alisa Lepselter **Kostüme:** Laura Cunningham Bauer **Musik:** Dick Hyman **Darsteller:** Anthony LaPaglia (*Al Torrio*); Brian Markinson (*Bill Shields*); Gretchen Mol (*Ellie*); Samantha Morton (*Hattie*); Sean Penn (*Emmet Ray*); Uma Thurman (*Blanche*); James Urbaniak (*Harry*); John Waters (*Mr. Haynes*); Tony Darrow (*Ben*); Brad Garrett (*Joe Bedloe*); Vincent Guastaferro (*Sid Bishop*); Denis O'Hare (*Jake*); Molly Price (*Ann*); Kaili Vernoff (*Gracie*); Chuck Lewkowicz (*Polizist*); Michael Sprague (*Django Reinhardt*); Woody Allen (*er selbst*); Ben Duncan (*er selbst*); Daniel Okrent (*A.J. Pickman*); Dan Moran (*Boss*); Chris Bauer (*Ace*); Constance Shulman (*Hazel*); Kellie Overbey (*Iris*); Darryl Alan Reed (*Don*); Marc Damon Johnson (*Omer*); Ron Cephas Jones (*Alvin*); Steve Bargonetti/Benjamin Franklin Brown (*Musikerfreunde*); Vince Giordano (*Bassist*); Emme Kemp/Clark Gayton/Marcus McLaurine (*Jam Session Musiker*); Carolyn Saxon (*Phyliss*); Drummond Erskine/Joe Ambrose (*Landstreicher*); Joe Rigano (*Bühnenarbeiter*); Dennis Stein (*Dick Ruth*); Net Hentoff (*er selbst*); Katie Hamill (*Mary*); Carole Bayeux (*Rita*); Paula Parish/Cory Solar/Lexi Egz/Yvette Mercedes/Peter Leung (*Partygäste*); William Addy (*Conférencier*); Dick Monday (*Chester Weems*); Mary Stout (*Amateursängerin Felicity Thomson*); Dick Mingalone (*Vogelstimmenimitator*); Mr. Spoons (*Löffelspieler*); Carol Woods (*Helen Minton*); Josh Mowery (*Kinodirektor*); Fred Goehner (*William Weston*); Eddy Davis (*2. Bassist*); Ralph Pope (*Bettler*); Douglas McGrath (*er selbst*); Jerome Richardson/Earl P. McIntyre/James Williams/Frank Wellington Wess/Al Bryant (*Club Musiker*); Ray Garvey (*Club Manager*); Sally Placksin (*Sally Jillian*); Lola Pashalinski (*Blanches Freundin*); Simon Wettenhall/Orange Kellin/Brooks Giles III (*Jam Session Musiker*); Alfred Sauchelli Jr. (*Ned*); Michael Bolus (*Lynch*); Mick O'Rourke/John P. McLaughlin (*schießende Ladendiebe*); Rick Mowat (*Mann mit Reifenpanne*); Ted Wilkins (*Tankstellenbesitzer*) *Ungenannt*[1]: Kenneth Edelson (*Partygast*)

Handlung: Das Porträt der fiktiven Dreißigerjahre-Jazzlegende Emmet Ray, der darunter leidet, nur der zweitbeste Gitarrist nach Django Reinhardt zu sein. Der Film hat die Form eines Dokudramas. Bekannte Jazzexperten, unter anderem Woody Allen selbst, erzählen Anekdoten über das ausschweifende Leben des egozentrischen Musikgenies, das geprägt war von Alkoholexzessen, Schulden und zahllosen Geliebten. Besonders übel spielt Emmet der stummen Wäscherin Hattie mit, die echte Gefühle für ihn hat. Erst sehr viel später erkennt er seinen Fehler... Der Film ist eine Hommage an den Gitarristen Django Reinhardt und die große Ära des Jazz und Swing.

Musiktitel: Robert Katscher/B. G. DeSylva: *When Day Is Done* • Larry Shields/Henry Ragas: *Clarinet Marmalade* • Jean Lenoir/Bruce Siever: *Speak To Me Of Love/Parlez-Moi D'Amour* • Django Reinhardt/Stéphane Grappelli: *Mystery Pacific* • Philip Braham/Douglas Furber: *Limehouse Blues* • Irving Mills/Duke Ellington: *It Don't Mean A Thing* • Johnny Green/Edward Heyman: *Out Of Nowhere* • Gus Kahn/Isham Jones: *I'll See You In My Dreams* • Ben Bernie/Kenneth Casey/Maceo Pinkard: *Sweet Georgia Brown* • Vincent Rose/Al Jolson/B. G. DeSylva: *Avalon* • Henry Creamer/Turner Layton: *After You've Gone* • James Brockman/Nathaniel Hawthorne Vincent/James Kendis/John William Kellette: *I'm Forever Blowing Bubbles* • Cecil Mack/Lew Brown/Ford Dabney: *Shine* • Billy Higgins/W. Benton Overstreet: *There'll Be Some Changes Made* • Clarence Williams/Sidney Bechet: *Viper Mad* • Ballard MacDonald/James F. Hanley: *Indiana* • Queen Lili' Uokalani: *Aloha Oe* • Henry Francis Lyte/William H. Monk: *Abide With Me* • Euday Bowman: *12th Street Rag* • Moises Simons/L. Wolfe Gilbert/Marion Sunshine: *The Peanut Vendor* • Gerald Marks/Seymour B. Simons: *All of Me* • Duke Ellington/Juan Tizol/Irving Mills: *Caravan* • James P. Johnson/Cecil Mack: *Old Fashioned Love* • Leonello Casucci/Irving Caesar/Julius Brammer: *Just A Gigolo* • Bert Kalmar/Harry Ruby: *Nevertheless* • Dick Hyman: *3:00 AM Blues*; *Unfaithful Woman* • Franz Liszt: *Liebestraum Nr. 3* • Ray Ludwig/Howdy Quicksell: *Since My Best Gal Turned Me Down* • Ted Koehler/Billy Moll/Harry Barris: *Wrap Your Troubles In Dreams* • Henry Busse/Henry Lange/Lou Davis: *Hot Lips* • Arthur Freed/Nacio Herb Brown: *You Were Meant For Me* • Harry Warren/Al Dubin: *Lulu's Back In Town* • Will J. Harris/Victor Young: *Sweet Sue, Just You*

2000

Schmalspurganoven
(*Small Time Crooks*)
USA, ca. 90 Minuten

Regie: Woody Allen **Drehbuch:** Woody Allen **Produktion:** Jean Doumanian **Kamera:** Fei Zhao **Schnitt:** Alisa Lepselter **Kostüme:** Suzanne McCabe **Musik:** s. Musiktitel **Darsteller:** Woody Allen (*Ray*); Tony Darrow (*Tommy*); Hugh Grant (*David*); George Grizzard (*George Blint*); Jon Lovitz (*Benny*); Elaine May (*May*); Michael Rapaport (*Denny*); Elaine Stritch (*Chi Chi Potter*); Tracey Ullman (*Frenchy*); Scotty Bloch (*Edgars Frau*); Brian Markinson (*Polizist*); Douglas McGrath/Peter McRobbie (*Frenchys Anwälte*); Isaac Mizrahi (*Winklers Chef*); Kristine Nielsen (*Emily Bailey*); Larry Pine (*Charles Bailey*); Carolyn Saxon (*Candy*); Sam Josepher (*Immobilienmakler*); Howard Erskine (*Langston Potter*); Lawrence Levy (*Dynamitverkäufer*); Diane Bradley/Crystal Field/Cindy Carver/Ray Garvey/Bill Gerber/Olivia Hayman/Laurine Towler/Fanda Nikic (*Kunden im Keksladen*); Dana Tyler (*TV-Reporterin*); Steve Kroft (*er selbst*); Brian McConnachie (*Paul Milton*); Riccardo Bertoni (*Winklers Butler*); Julie Lund (*Linda Rhinelander*); Teri Black/John Doumanian/Phyllis Burdoe (*Winklers Partygäste*); Maurice Sonnenberg (*Garth Steinway*); Richard Mawe (*Anthony Gwynne*); Karla Wolfangle/Rob Besserer (*Modern Dance Performer*); Frank Wood (*Oliver*); Ruth Laredo (*Konzertpianistin*); Julie Halston (*Konzert-Partygast*); Anthony Sinopoli (*Frenchys Chauffeur*); Jesse Levy (*Cellist in der Kirche*); Josephine Calabrese/Cindy Wilks/Trevor Moran (*Kirchgänger*); Christine Pipgras/Nick Garfinkle/Kenneth Edelson/Ira Wheeler/William Hill (*Potters Partygäste*); Ramsey Faragallah (*Potters Kellner*); Marvin Chatinover (*Dr. Henske*)

Handlung: Die Geschichte eines unerwarteten Aufstiegs: Während der Kleinkriminelle Ray und seine Kumpel vergeblich versuchen, einen Tunnel zum benachbarten Bankhaus zu graben, entwickelt sich die Bäckerei seiner Frau Frenchy, die eigentlich nur zur Tarnung eingerichtet wurde, zur Goldgrube…

Musiktitel: Al Dubin/Harry Warren: *With Plenty Of Money And You* • Stephen Lang: *Could It Be* • Edgar Sampson/Benny Goodman/Chick Webb: *Stompin' At The Savoy* • Harry James/Don Raye: *Music Makers* • Johann Strauß Sohn: *Frühlingsstimmen-Walzer* op. 410 • Sam Coslow/Arthur Johnston: *Cocktails For Two* • Chuck Río: *Tequila* • Scott Marshall: *The Modern Dance* • Sergei Rachmaninow: *Prélude b*-Moll op. 32 • Fermo Marchetti/Dick Manning: *Fascination* • Richard Rodgers/Lorenz Hart: *Mountain Greenery* • André Previn: *Zelda's Theme* • Johann Sebastian Bach: *Suite Nr. 2 für Violoncello Solo d*-Moll BWV 1008, 4. *Sarabande* • Lester Lanin: *Cha-Cha* • Steve Allen: *This Could Be The Start Of Something Big* • Betty Comden/Adolph Green/Jule Styne: *Just In Time* • E.Y. Harburg/Burton Lane: *Old Devil Moon* • Jack Owens: *The Hukilau Song* • Ronald Graham/Milton Schafer: *Steady, Steady*

2000

Ich Hab Doch Nur Meine Frau Zerlegt
(*Picking Up The Pieces*)
USA, ca. 95 Minuten

Regie: Alfonso Arau **Drehbuch:** Bill Wilson **Produktion:** Paul L. Sandberg **Kamera:** Vittorio Storaro **Schnitt:** Michael R. Miller **Kostüme:** Marilyn Matthews **Musik:** Ruy Folguera **Darsteller:** Woody Allen (*Tex Cowley*); Maria Grazia Cucinotta (*Desi*); Cheech Marin (*Bürgermeister*); David Schwimmer (*Pater Jerome*); Kiefer Sutherland (*Officer Bobo*); Alfonso Arau (*Dr. Amado*); Enrique Castillo (*Grasiento*); Danny De La Paz (*Taxifahrer*); Andy Dick (*Pater Buñuel*); Fran Drescher (*Schwester Frida*); Joseph Gordon-Levitt (*Flaco*); Elliott Gould (*Pater LaCage*); Eddie Griffin (*Sediento*); Mia Maestro (*Carla*); Lupe Ontiveros (*Constancia*); Lou Diamond Phillips (*Officer Alfonso*); Pepe Serna (*Florencio*); Angélica Aragón (*Dolores*); Jorge Cervera Jr. (*Unojo*); O'Neal Compton (*Texas-John*); Richard Edson (*Edsel Farkus*); Jackie Guerra (*Meche*); Jon Huertas (*Paulo*); Kathy Kinney (*Mrs. Tattler*); Tony Plana (*Usher*); Richard C. Sarafian (*Wino*); Cecilia Tijerina (*Leticia*); Brian Brophy (*CNN Reporter*); Betty Carvalho (*Juana*); Marcus Demian (*Ricardo*); Jeannine De La Torre (*junge mexikanische Mutter*); Darius Grace (*Paco*); Miguel Mas (*Arbeiter*); Fritz Mashimo (*Japanischer Pilger*); Kit McDonough (*Tourist aus Alabama*); Dyana Ortelli (*Gaga*); Barbara Pilavin (*alte Wundersucherin*); Andrew Roa (*Investor*); Valente Rodriguez (*Cuetero*); Sharon Stone (*Candy*); Daisy White (*Conchata Ortiz*); Dana Woods (*Pequeño*)

Handlung: Der Metzger Tex Cowley hat in einem Anfall von Eifersucht seine Ehefrau Candy umgebracht und ihre Leiche zerlegt. Auf dem Weg nach New Mexico, wo Tex die Leiche begraben möchte, fällt eine Hand vom Wagen und wird von einer blinden Frau gefunden, die daraufhin wieder sehen kann. Schnell entsteht ein Reliquienkult um Candys Hand, und die cleveren Bewohner verwandeln ihren verschlafenen Ort umgehend in ein Wallfahrtszentrum. Tex versucht die Hand wieder an sich zu bringen, denn Officer Bobo ist ihm auf den Versen, und dem könnte die Hand bekannt vorkommen…

Musiktitel: Ron Morales/M. Spindola: *Bad Corazon En Pedazos* • Michael Morales/Felicia Morales: *Gente* • Michael Morales/Ron Morales: *Ultimo Amor*

2001

Im Bann Des Jade Skorpions
(*The Curse Of The Jade Scorpion*)
USA, ca. 97 Minuten

Regie: Woody Allen **Drehbuch:** Woody Allen **Produktion:** Letty Aronson **Kamera:** Fei Zhao **Schnitt:** Alisa Lepselter **Kostüme:** Suzanne McCabe **Musik:** s. Musiktitel **Darsteller:** Woody Allen (*C.W. Briggs*); Dan Aykroyd (*Chris Magruder*); Helen Hunt (*Betty Ann Fitzgerald*); Brian Markinson (*Al*); Wallace Shawn (*George Bond*); David Ogden Stiers (*Voltan*); Charlize Theron (*Laura Kensington*); Elizabeth Berkley (*Jill*); Peter Gerety (*Ned*); John Schuck (*Mize*); John Tormey (*Sam*); Kaili Vernoff (*Rosie*); Maurice Sonnenberg/John Doumanian (*Büroangestellte*); Kevin Cahoon (*Lieferservice*); Philip Levy (*Rockys Kellner*); Vince Giordano/Howard Alden/Ted Sommer/Randy Sandke/Peter Ecklund/Joel Helleny/Chuck Wilson/Ray Beckenstein/Lawrence Feldman/Ken Peplowski (*Rainbow Room All Stars*); Dick Hyman (*Band Leader*); Carole Bayeux (*Voltans Assistentin*); Kenneth Edelson/Brian McConnachie/Judy Gold (*Voltans Freiwillige*); Herb Lovelle (*Nachtwache*); Carmen (*Rose Kensington*); Patrick Horgan/Howard Erskine/Ira Wheeler/Tina Sloan (*Kensington Gäste*); Ramsey Faragallah (*Detektiv*); Bob Dorian (*Mike*); Arthur Nascarella (*Tom*); Trude Klein (*Kensington Angestellte*); Prof. Irwin Corey (*Charlie*); Michael Mulheren (*Herb Coopersmith*); Peter Linari (*Joe Coopersmith*); Ray Garvey (*Polizist in der Wache*); Bruce Brown (*Radioansager*); Dan Moran (*Straßenkontakt*)

Handlung: New York in den 40er Jahren: der erfolgreiche Versicherungsdetektiv Briggs lässt sich auf einer Party vom Magier Voltan mit Hilfe eines Skorpionpendels in Trance versetzen. Mit diesem scheinbar harmlosen Trick wird Briggs zum Werkzeug von Gangstern, die ihn auf Juwelenraub schicken, ohne dass er sich später daran erinnern kann. Nun muss er also das Verbrechen aufklären, dass er selber begangen hat. Zu allem Überfluss hat er es dabei mit der neuen, ihm verhassten Kollegin Betty Ann Fitzgerald zu tun. Schon bald verdächtigen sich die beiden gegenseitig…

Musiktitel: Duke Ellington/Mitchell Parish/Irving Mills: *Sophisticated Lady* • Frank Loesser/Hoagy Charmichael: *Two Sleepy People* • Buddy Feyne/William Johnson/Julian Dash/Erskine Hawkins: *Tuxedo Junction* • Nancy Hamilton/Morgan Lewis: *How High The Moon* • Albert W. Ketèlbey: *In A Persian Market* • Harry James: *Flatbush Flanagan* • Frankie Carle/Jack Lawrence: *Sunrise Serenade*

2002

Hollywood Ending
(*Hollywood Ending*)
USA, ca. 107 Minuten

Regie: Woody Allen **Drehbuch:** Woody Allen **Produktion:** Letty Aronson **Kamera:** Wedigo von Schultzendorff **Schnitt:** Alisa Lepselter **Kostüme:** Melissa Toth **Musik:** s. Musiktitel **Darsteller:** Woody Allen (*Val*); George Hamilton (*Ed*); Téa Leoni (*Ellie*); Debra Messing (*Lori*); Mark Rydell (*Al*); Treat Williams (*Hal*); Peter Gerety (*Psychiater*); Erica Leerhsen (*Schauspielerin*); Jodie Markell (*Andrea Ford*); Isaac Mizrahi (*Elio Sebastian*); Marian Seldes (*Alexandra*); Aaron Stanford (*Schauspieler*); Tiffani Thiessen (*Sharon Bates*); Mark Webber (*Tony Waxman*); Bob Dorian/Ivan Martin/Gregg Edelman/Mary Schmidtberger (*Galaxie-Chefs*); Neal Huff (*Werbefilmer*); Douglas McGrath/Stephanie Roth Haberle/Bill Gerber/Roxanne Perry (*Barbeque Gäste*); Barbara Carroll (*Pianistin im Carlyle*); Howard Erskine (*Gast im Carlyle*); Yu Lu (*Kameramann*); Barney Cheng (*Übersetzer*); Anthony Arkin/Ramsey Faragallah (*Vorsprecher*); Olivia Hayman (*Balthazar-Empfangsdame*); Peter Van Wagner/Judy Toma (*Balthazar-Paar*); Sarah Polen/Amanda Jacobi/Steve Hurwitz/Ruth Last/Robert Lloyd Wolchok/Joel Eidelsberg (*Sedergäste*); Kenneth Edelson (*Augenarzt*); Ted Neustadt (*Röntgenarzt*); Reiko Takahashi (*Statist*); Greg Mottola (*Regieassistent*); Fred Melamed (*Pappas*); Jeff Mazzola (*Requisiteur*); Ray Garvey (*Techniker am Set*); Rochelle Oliver (*Script-Girl*); Joe Rigano (*Filmvorführer*); Maurice Sonnenberg (*Conférencier*)

Handlung: Regisseur Val Waxman hat seine beste Zeit lange hinter sich und verdient sein Geld als Werbefilmer. Eines Tages wird er wieder für eine teure Mainstream Produktion engagiert, an der pikanterweise auch seine Ex-Frau Elli und deren neue Liebe, der Produzent Hal Jaeger mitwirken. Das Projekt droht zu scheitern, als Val plötzlich an psychosomatisch bedingter Blindheit leidet...

Musiktitel: Arthur Freed/Nacio Herb Brown: *Going Hollywood* • Walter Donaldson/Harold Adamson: *It's Been So Long* • Richard A. Whiting/Johnny Mercer: *Hooray For Hollywood* • David Mann/Redd Evans: *No Moon At All* • Gus Arnheim/Charles N. Daniels/Harry Tobias: *Sweet And Lovely* • Jerry Bock/Larry Holofcener/George David Weiss: *Too Close For Comfort* • Raymond Hubbell/John Golden: *Poor Butterfly* • Harry Warren/Mack Gordon: *Serenade In Blue* • Chico O'Farrill: *Descarga* • Ivan De Prume/Shauna Reynolds/Jay Yuenger/Rob Zombie: *Grindhouse*

2003

Anything Else
(*Anything Else*)
USA, ca. 108 Minuten

Regie: Woody Allen **Drehbuch:** Woody Allen **Produktion:** Letty Aronson **Kamera:** Darius Khondji **Schnitt:** Alisa Lepselter **Kostüme:** Laura Jean Shannon **Musik:** s. Musiktitel
Darsteller: Woody Allen (*David Dobel*); Jason Biggs (*Jerry Falk*); Stockard Channing (*Paula*); Danny DeVito (*Harvey*); Jimmy Fallon (*Bob*); Christina Ricci (*Amanda*); Anthony Arkin (*Pip's Komiker*); David Conrad (*Dr. Reed*); Adrian Grenier (*Ray Polito*); William Hill (*Psychiater*); Erica Leerhsen (*Connie*); Fisher Stevens (*Manager*); Joseph Lyle Taylor (*Bill*); KaDee Strickland (*Brooke*); Diana Krall (*sie selbst*); Maurice Sonnenberg (*Kinodirektor*); Kenneth Edelson (*Rezeptionist*); Anthony J. Ribustello/Ray Garvey (*Schläger*); Wynter Kullman (*Emily*); Zach McLarty (*Ralph*); Ralph Pope (*Taxifahrer*); Manny Siverio/Jay Carrado (*Stunts*)

Handlung: Der junge Jerry Falk hat nur mäßigen Erfolg als Autor für Komiker. Deshalb ist er auch schon seit längerer Zeit mit seinem Agenten nicht mehr zufrieden, schafft es aber nicht, sich von ihm zu lösen. Auch die Beziehung zu seiner launischen Freundin Amanda wird immer schwieriger. Zufällig lernt Jerry in der Agentur den exzentrischen David Dobel kennen, einen Lehrer und Gelegenheitsautor. Der vierzig Jahre Ältere wird zu seinem väterlichen Mentor, denn er möchte Jerry dazu bringen, sein Leben endlich selbst in die Hand zu nehmen…

Musiktitel: Cole Porter: *Easy To Love* • Ravi Shankar: *Gat It* • Johnny Burke/Jimmy Van Heusen: *It Could Happen To You* • Herb Magidson/Allie Wrubel: *Gone With The Wind* • Jerome Kern/Dorothy Fields: *The Way You Look Tonight* • Clarence Gaskill/Jimmy McHugh: *I Can't Believe That You're In Love With Me* • Andy Razaf/Fats Waller: *Honeysuckle Rose* • Vernon Duke/Ira Gershwin: *I Can't Get Started* • Moby & Sylvia Robinson: *Sunday* • Peggy Lee/Hubie Wheeler: *There'll Be Another Spring* • Harry Warren/Mack Gordon: *There Will Never Be Another You*

2004

Melinda Und Melinda
(*Melinda And Melinda*)
USA, ca. 95 Minuten

Regie: Woody Allen **Drehbuch:** Woody Allen **Produktion:** Letty Aronson **Kamera:** Vilmos Zsigmond **Schnitt:** Alisa Lepselter **Kostüme:** Judy Ruskin Howell **Musik:** s. Musiktitel **Darsteller:** Chiwetel Ejiofor *(Ellis)*; Will Ferrell *(Hobie)*; Jonny Lee Miller *(Lee)*; Radha Mitchell *(Melinda)*; Amanda Peet *(Susan)*; Chloë Sevigny *(Laurel)*; Wallace Shawn *(Sy)*; David Aaron Baker *(Steve)*; Arija Bareikis *(Sally)*; Josh Brolin *(Greg)*; Steve Carell *(Walt)*; Stephanie Roth Haberle *(Louise)*; Shalom Harlow *(Joan)*; Geoffrey Nauffts *(Bud)*; Zak Orth *(Peter)*; Larry Pine *(Max)*; Vinessa Shaw *(Stacey)*; Brooke Smith *(Cassie)*; Daniel Sunjata *(Billy)*; Neil Pepe *(Al)*; Michael J. Farina *(Mann mit Hund)*; Matt Servitto *(Jack)*; Andy Borowitz *(Doug)*; Christina Kirk *(Jennifer)*; Alyssa Pridham *(Schauspielschülerin)*; Katie Kreisler *(Regisseurin)*; Quincy Rose *(2. Regieassistent)*; Rick Vincent Holmes/Michele Durning *(Party Gäste)*; Yi-Wen Jiang/Honggang Li/Weigang Li/Nicholas Tzavaras *(Shanghai Quartet)*; Rob Buntzen *(Antiquitätenhändler)* **Ungenannt**[1]: Kenneth Edelson *(Discobesucher)*

Handlung: Die Geschichte von Melinda wird im Wechsel in zwei verschiedenen Varianten erzählt, einmal als Tragödie und einmal als Komödie. Ausgangspunkt sind jeweils eine Dinner Party, in die Melinda unerwartet platzt und ein Gastgeber-Paar, das versucht, Melinda an einen der Gäste zu verkuppeln… Ist das Leben nun tragisch oder komisch?

Musiktitel: Igor Strawinski: *Violinkonzert in D-Dur, 2. Arioso. Andantino* • Billy Strayhorn: *Take The 'A' Train* • Johann Sebastian Bach: *Partita Nr. 3 a-Moll BWV 827*; *Präludium Nr. 2 c-Moll BWV 847*, aus *Das Wohltemperierte Klavier* • Matt Dennis/Tom Adair: *Will You Still Be Mine* • Lew Brown/B. G. DeSylva/Ray Henderson: *The Best Things In Life Are Free* • Duke Ellington: *In A Mellow Tone* • Eddie DeLange/Jimmy Van Heusen: *Darn That Dream* • Will Hudson/Irving Mills/Eddie DeLange: *Moonglow* • David Mann/Redd Evans: *No Moon At All* • Victor Young/Ned Washington: *Love Me* • Eubie Blake/Andy Razaf: *Memories Of You* • Leo Wood: *Somebody Stole My Gal* • Béla Bartók: *Streichquartett Nr. 4 C-Dur Sz 91* • Bob Russell/Duke Ellington: *Don't Get Around Much Anymore* • Duke Ellington/Irving Mills/Henry Nemo/John Redmond: *I Let A Song Go Out Of My Heart* • James Harris III/Terry Lewis, James Wright, Barry White: *Come On* • Heinz Roemheld: *Cat Scream* • Johannes Brahms: *Sapphische Ode* op. 94 Nr. 4 • Bhooka/T-Bone: *Comin' At Ya* • Adam Hamilton: *Big Eternity*

2005

Match Point
(*Match Point*)
GB/USA/Luxemburg, ca. 119 Minuten

Regie: Woody Allen **Drehbuch:** Woody Allen **Produktion:** Letty Aronson/Gareth Wiley/Lucy Darwin **Kamera:** Remi Adefarasin **Schnitt:** Alisa Lepselter **Kostüme:** Jill Taylor **Musik:** s. Musiktitel **Darsteller:** Brian Cox (*Alec Hewett*); Matthew Goode (*Tom Hewett*); Scarlett Johansson (*Nola Rice*); Emily Mortimer (*Chloe Hewett Wilton*); Jonathan Rhys Meyers (*Chris Wilton*); Penelope Wilton (*Eleanor Hewett*); Ewen Bremner (*Inspector Dowd*); James Nesbitt (*Detective Banner*); Rupert Penry-Jones (*Henry*); Alexander Armstrong (*Mr. Townsend*); Paul Kaye (*Immobilienmakler*); Janis Kelly/Alan Oke („*La Traviata*"-*Darsteller*); Mark Gatiss (*Tischtennisspieler*); Philip Mansfield (*Kellner*); Simon Kunz (*Rod Carver*); Geoffrey Streatfield (*Alan Sinclair*); Mary Hegarty („*Rigoletto*"-*Darsteller*); John Fortune (*John der Chauffeur*); Patricia Whymark (*Telefonvermittlerin*); Anthony O'Donnell (*Hausmeister*); Miranda Raison (*Heather*); Rose Keegan (*Carol*); Zoe Telford (*Samantha*); Margaret Tyzack (*Mrs. Eastby*); Scott Handy/Emily Gilchrist (*Hewetts Freunde*); Selina Cadell (*Margaret*); Georgina Chapman (*Nolas Kollegin*); Colin Salmon (*Ian*); Toby Kebbell (*Polizist*); Steve Pemberton (*Detective Parry*)

Handlung: Match Point ist der erste Film, den Woody Allen in Europa gedreht hat. London wählt er als Schauplatz für die Geschichte des ambitionierten Tennislehrers Chris Wilton, der, aus kleinen Verhältnissen stammend, seine Kontakte zur Upper Class für einen kometenhaften Aufstieg nutzt. Er heiratet die Tochter der reichen Familie Hewitt, seine Leidenschaft aber gilt der erfolglosen Schauspielerin Nora Rice. Als Nora ihm eröffnet, dass sie schwanger ist, muss Chris um seinen neuen, liebgewonnenen Lebensstil bangen…

Musiktitel: Gaetano Donizetti: *Una furtiva lagrima*, aus der Oper *Der Liebestrank* • Giuseppe Verdi: *Un di felice, eterea*, aus der Oper *La Traviata*; *Mal reggendo all'aspro assalto*, aus der Oper *Il Trovatore*; *Gualtier Maldè! ...Caro nome che il mio cor*, aus der Oper *Rigoletto*; *Desdemona*, aus der Oper *Otello*; *O figli, o figli miei!* aus der Oper *Macbeth* • Salvator Rosa: *Mia Piccirella* • Georges Bizet: *Mi par d'udir ancora*, aus der Oper *Die Perlenfischer* • Giacomo Rossini: *Arresta!* aus der Oper *Wilhelm Tell* • Andrew Lloyd Webber: *I Believe My Heart*, aus dem Musical „*The Woman In White*"

2006

Scoop – Der Knüller
(*Scoop*)
GB/USA, ca. 90 Minuten

Regie: Woody Allen **Drehbuch:** Woody Allen **Produktion:** Letty Aronson/Gareth Wiley **Kamera:** Remi Adefarasin **Schnitt:** Alisa Lepselter **Kostüme:** Jill Taylor **Musik:** s. Musiktitel **Darsteller:** Woody Allen (*Sid Waterman „Splendini"/Mr. Spence*); Hugh Jackman (*Peter Lyman*); Scarlett Johansson (*Sondra Pransky/Jade Spence*); Ian McShane (*Joe Strombel*); Charles Dance (*Mr. Malcom*); Romola Garai (*Vivian*); Kevin R. McNally (*Mike Tinsley*); Jim Dunk (*Trauerredner*); Robert Bathurst/Geoff Bell/Christopher Fulford/Nigel Lindsay (*Strombles Kollegen*); Fenella Woolgar (*Jane Cook*); Peter Mastin (*Tod*); Doreen Mantle/David Schneider/Meera Syal (*Joes Mitfahrer*); Robin Kerr/Richard Stirling (*Tinsleys Fans*); Carolyn Backhouse (*Vivians Mutter*); Guo Toa (*Jar Spinner*); Sam Friend (*Vivians Bruder*); Mark Heap (*M.C.*); Suzy Kewer (*Splendinis Assistentin*); Jody Halse (*Bühnenarbeiter*); Matt Day (*Jerry Burke*); Elizabeth Berrington (*Frau im Antiquitätenladen*); Rupert Frazer (*Mann im Antiquitätenladen*); Christopher Godwin (*Empfangsmitarbeiter*); Julian Glover (*Lord Lyman*); Paula Wilcox/John Standing (*Gartenparty-Gäste*); Sanjeev Bhasker/John Light (*Pokerspieler*); Tina Rath (*Wendy Beamish*); Caroline Blakiston/Richard Johnson (*Mr. u. Mrs. Quincy*); William Hoyland (*Butler*); Moya Brady (*schreiende Frau*); Rosie Cavaliero/Anthony O'Donnell (*Passanten*); Lynda Baron/Phil Cornwell (*Mieter*); Victoria Hamilton (*Jan*); Meg Wynn Owen (*Haushälterin*); Alexander Armstrong (*Polizist*); Anthony Head (*Detective*); Julia Deakin/Margaret Tyzack/Jeffry Wickham (*Sids Mitfahrer*)

Handlung: Der kürzlich verstorbene Reporter Joe Strombel ist mit seinen Begleitern auf dem Totenschiff unterwegs ins Jenseits. Mit dabei ist auch Jane Cook, die ehemalige Sekretärin des Adligen Peter Lyman. Sie erzählt Strombel von ihrem Verdacht, ihr Chef habe sie vergiftet, da sie einem dunklen Geheimnis auf die Spur gekommen sei: Lyman ist wahrscheinlich der sogenannte Tarotkarten-Serienmörder, der bereits etliche Frauen in London auf dem Gewissen hat. Diesen „Knüller" möchte sich Strombel nicht entgehen lassen, und tatsächlich gelingt es ihm, das Schiff vorrübergehend zu verlassen. Er taucht in der Entmaterialisierungskabine des Magiers Sid Waterman wieder auf und trifft dort auf die Studentin Sondra Pransky, die von Waterman für dessen Trick auf die Bühne geholt wurde. Strombel bittet Sondra, die Auflösung des Falls an seiner Stelle weiterzuverfolgen. Nach anfänglichen Zweifeln ist auch Sid bereit, Sondra dabei zu helfen…

Musiktitel: Peter Tschaikowski: *Suite* op. 20a, 3. *Tanz der Schwäne*, aus dem Ballett *Schwanensee*; *Suite* op. 71a, aus dem Ballett *Der Nussknacker* • Johann Strauß Sohn: *Annen-Polka* op. 117; *Tritsch-Tratsch-Polka* op. 214 • Irving Fields/Albert Gamse/John A. Camacho: *Miami Beach Rumba* • Aram Chatschaturjan: *Säbeltanz*, aus dem Ballett *Gayaneh* • Edvard Grieg: *Suite Nr. 1* op. 46, 4. *In Der Halle Des Bergkönigs*, aus dem Bühnenstück *Peer Gynt* • J. Sanders: *Adios Muchachos* • Luiz António/Djalma Ferreira: *Recado* • Ernesto Nazareth/Domenico Savino: *Dengozo*

2007

Cassandras Traum
(Cassandra's Dream)
USA/GB/Frankreich, ca. 104 Minuten

Regie: Woody Allen **Drehbuch:** Woody Allen **Produktion:** Letty Aronson/Stephen Tenenbaum/Gareth Wiley **Kamera:** Vilmos Zsigmond **Schnitt:** Alisa Lepselter **Kostüme:** Jill Taylor **Musik:** Philip Glass **Darsteller:** Hayley Atwell (*Angela*); Colin Farrell (*Terry*); Sally Hawkins (*Kate*); Ewan McGregor (*Ian*); Tom Wilkinson (*Howard*); John Benfield (*Vater*); Phil Davis (*Martin Burns*); Peter Hugo Daly (*Bootsbesitzer*); Clare Higgins (*Mutter*); Ashley Madekwe (*Lucy*); Andrew Howard (*Jerry*); Keith Smee (*Terrys Kumpel*); Stephen Noonan (*Mel*); Dan Carter (*Fred*); Richard Lintern (*Direktor*); Jennifer Higham (*Helen*); Lee Whitlock (*Mike*); Michael Harm (*Immobilienmakler*); Hugh Rathbone/Allan Ramsey/Paul Davis/Terry Budin Jones/Franck Viano/Tommy Mack/Milo Bodrozic (*Pokerspieler*); Emily Gilchrist (*Dora*); George Richmond (*Bernard*); Phyllis Roberts (*Burns Mutter*); Tamzin Outhwaite (*Burns Date*); Cate Fowler/David Horovitch (*Angelas Eltern*); Matt Bardock (*Jaguarbesitzer*); Jim Carter (*Chef der Autowerkstatt*); Tom Fisher (*Nigel*); Paul Gardner (*Bentleyverkäufer*); Mark Umbers (*Eisley*); Maggie McCarthy (*Dienstmädchen*); Richard Graham/Ross Boatman (*Detektive*) Ungenannt**Fehler! Textmarke nicht definiert.**: Kenneth Edelson (*Tim, Drehbuchautor*)

Handlung: Die Brüder Ian und Terry leben in London in einfachen Verhältnissen. Mit dem Gewinn aus einem Hunderennen kaufen sie gemeinsam ein Segelboot, das sie „Cassandras Traum" nennen. Ihre Geldsorgen verschärfen sich, als Terry beim Pokerspiel verliert und Ian seiner neuen, anspruchsvollen Freundin imponieren möchte. So bitten sie ihren reichen Onkel Howard um Hilfe. Howard stellt allerdings eine Bedingung: Ian und Terry sollen seinen Geschäftspartner beseitigen…

Musiktitel: H. Salters: *Time To Undress* • Kemdi Amadiume/Regis Godon: *You've Got It* • Irving King/Hal Swaine: *Show Me The Way To Go Home* • Michael Goldwasser/Josh Kessler/Marc Ferrari: *Giving You My Everything* • Edgard E. Jaude/Sophia Kartadinata-Levy/Philip G. Levy: *Infectious*

2008

Vicky Christina Barcelona
(*Vicky Christina Barcelona*)
USA/Spanien, ca. 92 Minuten

Regie: Woody Allen **Drehbuch:** Woody Allen **Produktion:** Letty Aronson/Stephen Tenenbaum/Gareth Wiley **Kamera:** Javier Aguirresarobe **Schnitt:** Alisa Lepselter **Kostüme:** Sonia Grande **Musik:** Philip Glass **Darsteller:** Javier Bardem (*Juan Antonio*); Patricia Clarkson (*Judy*); Penélope Cruz (*María Elena*); Kevin Dunn (*Mark*); Rebecca Hall (*Vicky*); Scarlett Johansson (*Cristina*); Chris Messina (*Doug*); Zak Orth (*Adam*); Carrie Preston (*Sally*); Pablo Schreiber (*Ben*); Christopher Evan Welch (*Erzähler*); Julio Perillán (*Charles*); Juan Quesada (*Gitarrist in Barcelona*); Ricard Salom/Maurice Sonnenberg (*Gäste der Kunstgalerie*); Manel Barceló (*Arzt*); Josep Maria Domènech (*Julio*); Emilio de Benito (*Gitarrist in Asturias*); Jaume Montané/Lloll Bertrán/Joel Joan/Sílvia Sabaté (*Juan Antonios Freunde*); Abel Folk (*Jay*)

Handlung: Die beiden Freundinnen Vicky und Christina verbringen einen Sommer im Haus von Bekannten in Barcelona. Bei einer Vernissage lernen sie den Maler Juan kennen. Juan lädt die beiden mit sehr eindeutigen Absichten auf sein Hotelzimmer ein. Vicky, die in Kürze heiraten will, ist darüber empört. Ihrer Freundin zuliebe willigt sie aber schließlich ein, ein Wochenende zu dritt in Juans Landhaus zu verbringen. Dort entwickeln sich die Dinge dann ganz anderes als geplant…

Musiktitel: Giulia Tellarini/Maik Alemany/Alejandro Mazzoni/Jens Neumaier: *Barcelona*; *La Ley Del Retiro* • Isaac Albéniz: *Asturias*; *Granada* • Juan Serrano: *Gorrion*; *Entre Las Olas* • Paco de Lucía/José Torregrosa: *Entre Dos Aguas* • Catalanisches Volkslied: *El Noi De La Mare* • Biel Ballester: *When I Was A Boy*; *Your Shining Eyes* • Stephane Wrembel: *Big Brother*

2009

Whatever Works – Liebe Sich Wer Kann
(*Whatever Works*)
USA/Frankreich, ca. 88 Minuten

Regie: Woody Allen **Drehbuch:** Woody Allen **Produktion:** Letty Aronson/Stephen Tenenbaum **Kamera:** Harris Savides **Schnitt:** Alisa Lepselter **Kostüme:** Suzy Benzinger **Musik:** s. Musiktitel **Darsteller:** Ed Begley Jr. (*John*); Patricia Clarkson (*Marietta*); Larry David (*Boris*); Conleth Hill (*Brockman*); Evan Rachel Wood (*Melody*); Henry Cavill (*Randy*); John Gallagher Jr. (*Perry*); Jessica Hecht (*Helena*); Carolyn McCormick (*Jessica*); Christopher Evan Welch (*Howard*); Adam Brooks/Lyle Kanouse/Michael McKean (*Boris' Freunde*); Clifford Lee Dickson (*Junge auf der Straße*); Yolonda Ross (*Mutter des Jungen*); Samantha Bee (*Schach-Mutter*); Marcia DeBonis (*Frau im Chinesischen Restaurant*); Willa Cuthrell-Tuttleman (*Schach-Mädchen*); Nicole Patrick (*Perrys Freundin*); Lindsay Michelle Nader/Armand Schultz (*TV-Stimmen*); Olek Krupa (*Morgenstern*) *Ungenannt*[1]*:* Kenneth Edelson (*Galeriebesucher*)

Handlung: Manchmal bringt das Schicksal Menschen zusammen, wie sie nicht gegensätzlicher sein könnten – aber Hauptsache, es funktioniert… Eine typische Woody-Allen-Rolle übernimmt in diesem Film der Schauspieler Larry David: Er verkörpert den hypochondrisch-misanthropischen Physikprofessor Boris Yellnikoff, der sich wider Erwarten in die junge und ziemlich naive Ausreißerin Melody verliebt. Aber auch für einige andere Paare hält das Schicksal Überraschungen parat…

Musiktitel: Bert Kalmer/Harry Ruby: *Hello I Must Be Going* • Ludwig van Beethoven: *Sinfonie Nr. 9 (Ode an die Freude) d*-Moll op. 125, *2. Molto vivace*; *Sinfonie Nr. 5 (Schicksals-Sinfonie) c*-Moll op. 67 • Ray Ronnei: *Salty Bubble* • Heinz Kiessling: *Butterfly By* • Mildred J. Hill/Patty S. Hill: *Happy Birthday To Yo* • Werner Tautz: *Honeymoon Swoon* • Henry Creamer/James P. Johnson: *If I Could Be With You* • Kent Bucchanon: *Buttmeat Boogie* • Paul Taylor/Angela Maria Engelman: *Tonight* • Felix Mendelssohn-Bartholdy: *Hochzeitsmarsch*, aus *Ein Sommernachtstraum* op. 61 Nr. 7 • Antonio Carlos Jobim/Newton Mendonça: *Desafinado* • Frank Loesser: *Spring Will Be A Little Late This Year* • Luiz Floriano Bonfá/Maria Helena De Toledo/Giorgio Calabrese: *Menina Flor* • Traditionelles Neujahrslied: *Auld Lang Syne*

2010

Ich Sehe Den Mann Deiner Träume
(*You Will Meet A Tall Dark Stranger*)
USA/Spanien, ca. 98 Minuten

Regie: Woody Allen **Drehbuch:** Woody Allen **Produktion:** Letty Aronson/Stephen Tenenbaum/Jaume Roures **Kamera:** Vilmos Zsigmond **Schnitt:** Alisa Lepselter **Kostüme:** Beatrix Aruna Pasztor **Musik:** s. Musiktitel **Darsteller:** Antonio Banderas (*Greg*); Josh Brolin (*Roy*); Anthony Hopkins (*Alfie*); Gemma Jones (*Helena*); Freida Pinto (*Dia*); Lucy Punch (*Charmaine*); Naomi Watts (*Sally*); Pauline Collins (*Cristal*); Rupert Frazer (*Jogging Partner*); Kelly Harrison (*Personal Trainer*); Eleanor Gecks (*Inlineskater-Freundin*); Fenella Woolgar (*Jane*); Ewen Bremner (*Henry Strangler*); Christian McKay/Philip Glenister/Jonathan Ryland/Pearce Quigley (*Pokerfreunde*); Neil Jackson (*Alan*); Lynda Baron (*Alfies Date*); Robert Portal (*Schmuckverkäufer*); Jim Piddock (*Peter Wicklow*); Celia Imrie (*Enid Wicklow*); Roger Ashton-Griffiths (*Jonathan*); Anna Friel (*Iris*); Theo James (*Ray*); Christopher Fulford/Johnny Harris (*Rays Freunde*); Alex Macqueen (*Malcolm Dodds*); Anupam Kher/Meera Syal (*Dias Eltern*); Joanna David/Geoffrey Hutchings (*Alans Eltern*); Natalie Walker (*Alans Schwester*); Shaheen Khan (*Dias Tante*); Amanda Lawrence (*Medium*); Zak Orth (*Erzähler*)

Handlung: Als Helena von ihrem Mann Alfie nach 40 Jahren verlassen wird, wendet sie sich in ihrer Verzweiflung an eine Wahrsagerin. Diese hat gute Nachrichten für Helena („Ich sehe den Mann deiner Träume"), aber auch jede Menge ungebetene Ratschläge für die übrige Familie, die Helena nur zu gerne weitergibt. Zum Beispiel an Tochter Sally, die in ihrer Ehe mit dem erfolglosen Schriftsteller Roy nicht mehr glücklich ist. Um die Familie finanziell über Wasser zu halten nimmt Sally eine Stelle bei dem attraktiven Galeristen Greg an, während Roy sich in seine Schwärmerei für die Nachbarin von gegenüber flüchtet…

Musiktitel: Ned Washington/Leigh Harline: *When You Wish Upon A Star* • Ted Lewis/Bill Munro/Andrew B. Sterling/Harry von Tilzer: *When My Baby Smiles At Me* • Jimmy Campbell/Reg Connelly/Ted Shapiro: *If I Had You* • Luigi Boccherini: *Gitarrenquintett Nr. 4 (Fandango) D-Dur G 448, 3. Grave Assai* • Gus Kahn/Isham Jones: *I'll See You In My Dreams* • Marc Ferrari/Michael McGregor: *Let Your Body Move* • Wolfgang Amadeus Mozart: *Serenade Nr. 6 (Serenata Notturna) D-Dur KV 239, 3. Rondo. Allegretto* • Buck Ram/Ande Rand: *Only You* • Gaetano Donizetti: *Tu che a Dio spiegasti l'ali*, aus der Oper *Lucia Di Lammermoor* • Silver/Sir Realist: *Laser Luxe* • Giulia Tellarini/Maik Alemany Usón/Alejandro Mazzoni/Jens Neumaier: *Mais Si L'Amour* • Scott Nickoley/Jamie Dunlap: *I Never Loved You* • Lew Brown/B. G. DeSylva/Ray Henderson: *My Sin*

2011

Midnight In Paris
(*Midnight In Paris*)
USA/Spanien, ca. 90 Minuten

Regie: Woody Allen **Drehbuch:** Woody Allen **Produktion:** Letty Aronson/Stephen Tenenbaum/Jaume Roures **Kamera:** Darius Khondji **Schnitt:** Alisa Lepselter **Kostüme:** Sonia Grande **Musik:** s. Musiktitel **Darsteller:** Kathy Bates (*Gertrude Stein*); Adrien Brody (*Salvador Dalí*); Carla Bruni (*Fremdenführerin*); Marion Cotillard (*Adriana*); Rachel McAdams (*Inez*); Michael Sheen (*Paul*); Owen Wilson (*Gil*); Nina Arianda (*Carol*); Kurt Fuller (*John*); Tom Hiddleston (*F. Scott Fitzgerald*); Mimi Kennedy (*Helen*); Alison Pill (*Zelda Fitzgerald*); Léa Seydoux (*Gabrielle*); Corey Stoll (*Ernest Hemingway*); Maurice Sonnenberg (*Mann bei der Weinprobe*); Thierry Hancisse/Guillaume Gouix/Audrey Fleurot/Marie-Sohna Condé (*20er Jahre Partygäste*); Yves Heck (*Cole Porter*); Sonia Rolland (*Joséphine Baker*); Daniel Lundh (*Juan Belmonte*); Laurent Spielvogel (*Antiquitätenhändler*); Thérèse Bourou-Rubinsztein (*Alice B. Toklas*); Marcial Di Fonzo Bo (*Pablo Picasso*); Emanuelle Uzan (*Djuna Barnes*); Tom Cordier (*Man Ray*); Adrien De Van (*Luis Buñuel*); Serge Bagdassarian (*Détective Duluc*); Gad Elmaleh (*Détective Tisserant*); David Lowe (*T. S. Eliot*); Atmen Kelif (*Hotelarzt*); Yves-Antoine Spoto (*Henri Matisse*); Laurent Claret (*Leo Stein*); Sava Lolov/Karine Vanasse (*Belle-Époque-Paar*); Catherine Benguigui (*Hostess im Maxim's*); Vincent Menjou Cortes (*Henri de Toulouse-Lautrec*); Olivier Rabourdin (*Paul Gauguin*); François Rostain (*Edgar Degas*); Marianne Basler/Michel Vuillermoz (*Versailles Königspaar*) Ungenannt[1]: Kenneth Edelson (*Gast im Maxim's*)

Handlung: Ein Amerikaner in Paris: Drehbuchautor Gil Pender, der lieber ein ernsthafter Schriftsteller wäre, reist mit seiner Verlobten und deren Eltern nach Paris. Während seine Begleiter die üblichen Besichtigungstouren absolvieren, liebt Gil vor allem die Atmosphäre der Stadt bei Regen und bei Nacht. Auf seinen Streifzügen durch die engen, dunklen Gassen erwacht vor seinen Augen das Paris der 20er Jahre, trifft er Ernest Hemingway, Cole Porter, Gertrude Stein und viele andere...

Musiktitel: Sidney Bechet/Jean Broussolle: *Si Tu Vois Ma Mère* • Rose Noel/Jean Casanova/Paul Durand: *Je Suis Seul Ce Soir* • Luiz António/Djalma Ferreira: *Recado* • Stephane Wrembel: *Bistro Fada* • Cole Porter: *Let's Do It*; *You've Got That Thing*; *You Do Something To Me* • A. Oréfiche/A. de Badet: *La Conga Blicoti* • Daniel May: *I Love Penny Sue* • James P. Johnson/Cecil Mack: *Charleston* • Milton Ager/Jack Yellen: *Ain't She Sweet* • Jean Lenoir: *Parlez-Moi D'Amour* • Jacques Offenbach: *Barcarolle*, aus der Oper *Hoffmanns Erzählungen*; *Can-Can*, aus der Oper *Orpheus In Der Unterwelt* • François Parisi: *Ballad Du Paris*; *Le Parc De Plaisir*

2012

Paris-Manhattan
(*Paris-Manhattan*)
F, ca. 75 Minuten

Regie: Sophie Lellouche **Drehbuch** Sophie Lellouche **Produktion:** Philippe Rousselet **Kamera:** Laurent Machuel **Schnitt:** Monica Coleman **Kostüme:** Fabienne Katany **Musik:** Jean-Michel Bernard **Darsteller:** Alice Taglioni (*Alice*); Patrick Bruel (*Victor*); Marine Delterme (*Hélène*); Michel Aumont (*Vater*); Louis-Do de Lencquesaing (*Pierre*); Marie-Christine Adam (*Mutter*); Jacques Herlin (*Mr. Aknin*); Yannick Soulier (*Vincent*); Margaux Châtelier (*Laura*); Gladys Cohen (*Mme Gozlan*); Arsène Mosca (*Arthur*); Julie Martel (*depressive Kundin*); Roman Guisset (*Dieb*); Juliette Kruh (*Alice' Assistentin*); Paul-Edouard Gondard (*Achille*); Jacques Ciron (*Präsident der Anwaltskammer*); Ariana Kah *(die letzte Kundin);* Christian Ameri (*der Kranke*); Khereddine Ennasri (*Kurier*); Raphaèl Delouya (*Junge mit Tretroller*); François Lescurat (*Concierge*); Jean-Jacques Albert (*Hoteldirektor*); David Marsais (*Mann auf der Kirmes*); Mohamed Lakhdar (*Saudi*); Jérôme Coué (*Mann mit Handy*); Caroline Gay (*Frau mit Mietfahrrad*); Mary Loy/Stéphane Poterlot/Paul Solas (*Hochzeitsmusiker*) *Ungenannt:* Woody Allen (*er selbst*)

Handlung: Die Apothekerin Alice Ovitz, Mitte dreißig und Single, ist schon seit ihrer Jugend ein großer Woody-Allen-Fan. Für die wichtigen Fragen ihres Lebens, vor allem auch die ihres Liebeslebens, sucht sie Antworten in den Lebensweisheiten seiner Filme. Denn mit allen anderen Männern tut sie sich eher schwer… Das Spielfilmdebut von Sophie Lellouche ist eine Hommage an Woody Allen, der auch selbst in einer kleinen Gastrolle auftritt, gespickt mit zahlreichen Filmzitaten.

Musiktitel: Christopher Franke: *Can I Have This Dance?* • Charles Harper: *Teenage* • Stephane Guillaume: *Night In Copacabana*; *Blue Note Bossa* • Declan Flynn: *Come Down* • Thomas Knight: *Somewhere There's A Someone* • Richard Rodgers/Lorenz Hart: *Bewitched* • Amilcare Ponchielli: *Suicido!...In questi fieri momenti*, aus der Oper *La Gioconda* • Cole Porter: *I'm In Love Again* • Johann Sebastian Bach: *Cembalokonzert f-Moll BWV 1056* • Frank Foster/Count Basie: *Back To The Apple* • Côme Aguiar: *Vincent*

2012

To Rome With Love
(*To Rome With Love*)
USA, ca. 107 Minuten

Regie: Woody Allen **Drehbuch:** Woody Allen **Produktion:** Letty Aronson/Stephen Tenenbaum/Giampaolo Letta/Faruk Alatan **Kamera:** Darius Khondji **Schnitt:** Alisa Lepselter **Kostüme:** Sonia Grande **Musik:** Goffredo Gibellini **Darsteller:** Woody Allen (*Jerry*); Alec Baldwin (*John*); Roberto Benigni (*Leopoldo*); Penélope Cruz (*Anna*); Judy Davis (*Phyllis*); Jesse Eisenberg (*Jack*); Greta Gerwig (*Sally*); Ellen Page (*Monica*); Antonio Albanese (*Luca Salta*); Fabio Armiliato (*Giancarlo, Michelangelos Vater*); Alessandra Mastronardi (*Milly*); Ornella Muti (*Pia Fusari*); Flavio Parenti (*Michelangelo*); Alison Pill (*Hayley*); Riccardo Scamarcio (*Hoteldieb*); Alessandro Tiberi (*Antonio*); Pierluigi Marchionne (*Verkehrspolizist*); Carol Alt (*Carol*); David Pasquesi (*Tim*); Lynn Swanson (*Ellen*); Monica Nappo (*Sofia*); Corrado Fortuna (*Rocco*); Margherita Vicario (*Claudia*); Rosa Di Brigida (*Mariangela*); Maurizio Argentieri (*Stimme des Piloten*); Giovanni Esposito (*Hotelangestellter*); Gabriele Rainone (*Gabriele*); Camilla Pacifico (*Camilla*); Massimo Ferroni/Alessandro Procoli/Paolo De Vita (*Leopolds Kollegen*); Cecilia Capriotti (*Serafina*); Duccio Camerini/Lina Sastri (*Freunde vor dem Kino*); Alberto Mangiante (*TV-Stimme*); Ruggero Cara/Maria Rosaria Omaggio/Giacomo Fadda (*Passanten*); Roberto Della Casa (*Onkel Paolo*); Ariella Reggio (*Tante Rita*); Gustavo Frigerio (*Onkel Sal*); Simona Caparrini (*Tante Giovanna*); Sergio Solli (*Leopoldos Chauffeur*); Cristiana Palazzoni (*TG3 Anchor Woman*); Massimo De Lorenzo (*Regisseur*); Giuseppe Pambieri (*Leopolds Chef*); Alessio Zucchini/Alessandro Tallarida (*Reporter in Leopoldos Büro*); Luca Calvani/Maricel Alvarez/Mariella Milani/Roberta Ronconi (*Reporter bei der Kinopremiere*); Marta Zoffoli (*Marisa Raguso*); Lino Guanciale (*Leonardo*); Fabio Bonini (*Max*); Brunella Matteucci (*Reporterin in Leopoldos Badezimmer*); Edoardo Leo (*Reporter beim Friseur*); Claudia Smith (*Modenschau-Model*); Antonio Rampino (*Oberkellner*); Anna Teresa Rossini/Gaetano Amato (*Paar im Restaurant*); Marina Rocco (*Tanya*); Sergio Bustric (*Mr. Massucci*); Augusto Fornari/Mariano Rigillo/Gianmarco Tognazzi (*Annas Kunden*); Ilaria Serrato (*Mädchen vor dem Friseurladen*); Vinicio Marchioni (*Aldo Romano*); Donatella Finocchiaro/Nusia Gorgone (*Reporterinnen auf der Straße*); Ninni Bruschetta/Carlo De Ruggieri (*Hoteldetektive*); Giuliano Gemma (*Hotelmanager*); Margherita Di Rauso (*Lucas Frau*); Federica Corti (*Mädchen mit Autogramm*); Rita Cammarano (*Nedda/Colombina* in der Oper *Bajazzo*); Matteo Bonotto (*Tonio, der Tölpel/Taddeo* in der Oper *Bajazzo*); Antonio Taschini (*Silvio* in der Oper *Bajazzo*); Vinicio Cecere (*Beppo/Harlekin* in der Oper *Bajazzo*); Francesco De Vito (*Mann im Fenster*)

Handlung: Ein Episodenfilm, der im Wechsel vier voneinander unabhängige Geschichten erzählt:

- Das amerikanische Ehepaar Phillis und Jerry (Psychiaterin und Opernregisseur im Ruhestand) reist in Rom an, um Michelangelo, den Verlobten ihrer Tochter kennenzulernen. Jerry entdeckt bald, dass Michelagelos Vater Giancarlo eine fantastische Singstimme hat und setzt nun alles daran, ihn auf eine Opernbühne zu bringen…

- Antonio und Milly, frisch verheiratet, wollen in Rom Verwandte von Antonio treffen, die ihm zu einer guten Stellung verhelfen können. Kaum angekommen, werden beide in amouröse Abenteuer verwickelt…

- Architekt John Foy befindet sich auf Urlaub in Rom. Durch die Begegnung mit Student Jack fühlt er sich in die Zeit zurückversetzt, die er selbst als junger Mann in Rom verlebt hat…

- Der Angestellte Leopoldo Pisanello wird aus unerklärlichen Gründen über Nacht zum Medienstar erkoren und erlebt alle Höhen und Tiefen des Ruhms…

Musiktitel: Domenico Modugno/Francesco Migliacci: *Volare* • Bruno Pallesi/Celso Valli/Paolo Zavallone: *Amada Mia, Amore Mio* • Pietro Garinei/Sandro Giovanni/Renato Ranucci: *Arrivederci Roma* • Alberto Pestalozza: *Ciribiribin* • Giacomo Puccini: *E lucevan le stelle*, aus der Oper *Tosca*; *Nessun dorma*, aus der Oper *Turandot* • Giovanni Vicari: *Mio Dolce Sogno* • Giovanni D'Anzi/Alfredo Bracchi: *Non Dimenticar Le Mie Parole* • Giuseppe Verdi: *Libiamo ne' lieti calici*, aus der Oper *La Traviata* • Umberto Giordano: *Amor ti vieta*, aus der Oper *Fedora* • Adam Hamilton: *Studio 99* • Alessandro Trebo/Andrea Benini: *Three Times Bossa* • Aaron Einar Swan: *When Your Lover Has Gone* • Ruggero Leoncavallo: *Son qua, son qua*; *Vesti la giubba*; *Duett* und *Finale*: jeweils aus der Oper *Bajazzo*

2013

Blue Jasmine
(*Blue Jasmine*)
USA, ca. 94 Minuten

Regie: Woody Allen **Drehbuch:** Woody Allen **Produktion:** Letty Aronson/Stephen Tenenbaum/Edward Walson **Kamera:** Javier Aguirresarobe **Schnitt:** Alisa Lepselter **Kostüme:** Suzy Benzinger **Musik:** Christopher Lennertz **Darsteller:** Alec Baldwin (*Harold „Hal" Francis*); Cate Blanchett (*Jeanette „Jasmine" Francis*); Louis C.K. (*Al*); Bobby Cannavale (*Chili, Gingers Verlobter*); Andrew Dice Clay (*Augie, Gingers Ex-Ehemann*); Sally Hawkins (*Ginger*); Peter Sarsgaard (*Dwight*); Michael Stuhlbarg (*Dr. Flicker*); Tammy Blanchard (*Jasmines Freundin Jane*); Max Casella (*Eddie*); Alden Ehrenreich (*Danny*); Joy Carlin (*Frau im Flugzeug*); Richard Conti (*Ehemann der Frau*); Glen Caspillo (*Taxifahrer*); Charlie Tahan (*junger Danny*); Annie McNamara (*Jasmines Freundin Nora*); Daniel Jenks (*Matthew*); Max Rutherford (*Johnny*); Kathy Tong (*Raylene*); Ted Neustadt/Andrew Long/Laurena Allan/John Harrington Bland/Leslie Lyles/Glenn Fleshler/Brynn Thayer/Christopher Rubin/Emily Bergl/Barbara Garrick (*Hals und Jasmines Freunde*); Ali Fedotowsky (*Melanie*); Dean Farwood (*Computerlehrer*); Conor Kellicutt/Colin Thomson (*Chilis Freunde*); Val Diamond/Joe Bellan/Catherine MacNeal/Irit Levi (*Zahnarztpatienten*); Diane Amos (*Zahnhygienikerin*); Shannon Finn (*Jasmins Freundin Sharon*); Tom Kemp (*Nat*); Emily Hsu (*Amy*); Maurice Sonnenberg (*Partygast*); Martin Cantu (*Gingers Chef*); Daniel Hepner (*Kellner im Café*); Al Palagonia (*U.S. Marshall*) Ungenannt[1]: Kenneth Edelson (*Partygast*); Donna Sue Jahier (*Café-Gast*)

Handlung: Nachdem ihr Mann Hal wegen Betrugs verhaftet wurde und sich im Gefängnis das Leben nahm, muss Society-Lady Jasmine ihr Luxusleben in New York aufgeben und notgedrungen zu ihrer Schwester nach San Francisco ziehen. Labil, und vom Tablettenmissbrauch gezeichnet, unternimmt sie eher halbherzige Schritte zu einem Neuanfang. Als der reiche Diplomat Dwight sich in Jasmine verliebt, scheint sich das Blatt noch einmal zu wenden… In den eingestreuten Rückblenden erfährt der Zuschauer die Hintergründe, die zu Jasmines Absturz geführt haben.

Musiktitel: Louis Armstrong/Luis Carl Russell: *Back O'Town Blues* • Clarence Williams/Joseph Oliver: *Speakeasy Blues* • Carey Morgan/Arthur M. Swanstrom/Charles R. McCarron: *Blues My Naughty Sweetie Gives To Me* • Eddie Green: *A Good Man Is Hard To Find* • Lorenz Hart/Richard Rodgers: *Blue Moon* • W.C. Handy: *Aunt Hagar's Blues* • Mezz Mezzrow/Sidney Bechet: *House Party* • Julius Block: *Great White Way*; *Yacht Club* • DJ Aljaro: *The Vision* • Paul Abler: *Ipanema Breeze* • Kully B/Gussy G/Bilkhu: *Out On The Town* • Bob Bradley/Matt Sanchez/Gavin McGrath: *Human Static* • Stephen Emil Dudas: *Average Joe* • Mireya und Raul Medina: *Miami Sunset Bar* • Andrew Bojanic/Wendy Page/James Fenton Marr: *Welcome To The Night* • David Chesky: *Love Theme* • J. Berni Barbour: *My Baby Sends Me* alias *My Daddy Rocks Me* • Clarence Williams/Joseph Oliver: *West End Blues* • Victoria Spivey: *Black Snake Swing* alias *Black Snake Blues*

2013

Plötzlich Gigolo
(*Fading Gigolo*)
USA, ca. 87 Minuten

Regie: John Turturro **Drehbuch:** John Turturro **Produktion:** Bill Block/Paul Hanson/Jeffrey Kusama-Hinte **Kamera:** Marco Pontecorvo **Schnitt:** Simona Paggi **Kostüme:** Donna Zakowska **Musik:** Abraham Laboriel/Bill Maxwell **Darsteller:** John Turturro (*Fioravante*); Woody Allen (*Murray*); Vanessa Paradis (*Avigal*); Liev Schreiber (*Dovi*); Sharon Stone (*Dr. Parker*); Sofía Vergara (*Selima*); M'Barka Ben Taleb (*Mimou*); Tonya Pinkins (*Othella*); David Margulies (*Chief Rebbe*); Abe Altman (*erster Rabbi*); Sol Frieder (*alter Rabbi*); Max Casella (*Mann am Schalter*); Loan Chabanol (*Loan*); Eugenia Kuzmina (*Straßenprostituierte*); Michael Badalucco (*dickleibiger Fahrer*); Aida Turturro (*Frau des Fahrers*); Allen Lewis Rickman (*Chassidischer Fahrer*); Jade Dixon (*Cee Cee*); Aubrey Joseph (*Cefus*); Dante Hoagland (*Coco*); Isaiah Clifton (*Cyrus*); Teddy Bergman (*Yossi*); Ness Krell (*kleine Devorah*); Russell Posner (*Malky*); Delphina Belle (*Rhuki*); Diego Turturro (*Shimshon*); Ted Sutherland (*Shmuel*); Hilma Falkowski (*Frau beim Lunch*); Salimatou Sillah (*Kellnerin*); Bob Balaban (*Sol*); Ungenannt[1]: Christine Vienna (*Society Lady*); Sherman Alpert (*Rabbi*); Ari Barkan (*Straßenreiniger mit Schlauch*); Joseph Basile (*Zuschauer beim Kidnapping*); Katherine Borowitz (*Englische Nachrichtensprecherin*); Aurélie Claudel (*Tai-Chi-Frau*); Elli (*Rabbi Elli*); Donna Sue Jahier (*Chassidische Nanny*); Anna Kuchma (*Mädchen am Telefon*); Fran Lieu (*Käuferin im Wäschegeschäft*); Jill Scott (*Rolle ungenannt*); Raymond Michael Bell (*Chassidischer Jude*)

Handlung: Der alte Buchhändler Murry muss seinen Laden schließen und blickt in eine ungewisse Zukunft. Als seine Hautärztin ihm anvertraut, dass sie mit ihrer Freundin einen Mann für einen flotten Dreier sucht, erkennt er sofort die Chance für ein lukratives Geschäft. So bringt er kurz entschlossen seinen jüngeren Freund, den Floristen Fioravante ins Spiel und bietet seinerseits Unterstützung bei der Beschaffung der weiblichen Kundschaft an, natürlich gegen entsprechende finanzielle Beteiligung. Fioravante zögert zunächst, doch schließlich wird aus dem einfühlsamen Floristen der Gigolo „Virgil". Der Erfolg lässt nicht lange auf sich warten - bis Fioravante die Liebe in die Quere kommt, und zwar in Gestalt der Rabbinerwitwe Avigal. Gleichzeitig bekommt es Murray mit der chassidischen Nachbarschaftspolizei zu tun…

Musiktitel: Norman Gimbel/Eddie Heywood: *Canadian Sunset* • José Padilla/Eduardo Montesinos: *La Violetera* • Troy Andrews: *Neph* • Robert „Pee Wee" Hill/Michiko Hill: *Pee Wee's Funk* • Bernice Petkere: *Close Your Eyes* • Lorenz Hart/Richard Rodgers: *My Romance* • Vincenzo De Crescenzo/Antonio Vian: *Luna Rossa* • Jack Wolf/Frank Sinatra/Joel Herron: *I'm A Fool To Want You* • Gene Ammons: *Blue Ammons* • Stefano Micarelli: *Reflejo De Luna* • Norman Gimbel/Pablo Beltrán Ruiz/Luis Demitrio Traconis Molina: *Sway* • L. Carmi/C.A. Liman/P. Delanoe/P. Havet: *Le Torrent* • Traditional: *Maggie Murphy's Home* • Domenico Modugno/Roberto Gigli: *Tu Si' 'Na Cosa Grande*

2014

Magic In The Moonlight
(*Magic In The Moonlight*)
USA, ca. 93 Minuten

Regie: Woody Allen **Drehbuch:** Woody Allen **Produktion:** Letty Aronson/Stephen Tenenbaum/Edward Walson **Kamera:** Darius Khondji **Schnitt:** Alisa Lepselter **Kostüme:** Sonia Grande **Musik:** s. Musiktitel **Darsteller:** Eileen Atkins (*Tante Vanessa*); Colin Firth (*Stanley*); Marcia Gay Harden (*Mrs. Baker*); Hamish Linklater (*Brice*); Simon McBurney (*Howard Burkan*); Emma Stone (*Sophie*); Jacki Weaver (*Grace*); Erica Leerhsen (*Caroline*); Catherine McCormack (*Olivia*); Jeremy Shamos (*George*); Antonia Clarke/Natasha Andrews/Valérie Beaulieu (*Wie Ling Soo's Assistentinnen*); Peter Wollasch (*Bühnenmanager*); Jürgen Zwingel/Wolfgang Pissors/Sébastien Siroux (*Fans hinter der Bühne*); Ute Lemper (*Cabaret Sängerin*); Didier Muller (*Butler*); Ronald Alphonse/Ronald Baker/Kelly Keto/Olivier Marchevet/Georges Édouard Nouel/Mark Sims (*Jazz Musiker*); Rudolf Krause/Patrick Zard/Pedro Chomnalez/Jessica Forde/Paul Bandey (*Reporter*); Lionel Abelanski (*Arzt*) *Ungenannt*[1]*:* Kenneth Edelson (*Gypsy*)

Handlung: Eine romantische Komödie um die junge Hellseherin Sophie, die in den 20er Jahren mit ihren übersinnlichen Fähigkeiten der dekadenten Oberschicht an der Côte d'Azur das Geld aus den Taschen zaubert. Nur der britische Gentleman Stanley, selbst ein erfolgreicher Magier, glaubt nicht an Geister und möchte der hübschen Schwindlerin zu gerne das Handwerk legen. Doch kann er Sophies's Charme widerstehen…?

Musiktitel: Cole Porter: *You Do Something To Me* • Igor Strawinski: *Die Anbetung der Erde,* aus dem Ballett *Le Sacre du Printemps (Frühlingsweihe)* • Maurice Ravel: *Boléro* • Ludwig van Beethoven: *Sinfonie Nr. 9 d-Moll, 2. Molto Vivace* • Mischa Spoliansky/Marcellos Schiffer: aus der Revue *Alles Schwindel* • Kurt Weill/Bertolt Brecht: *Die Moritat Von Mackie Messer,* aus der *Dreigroschenoper* • Joseph A. Burke/Al Dubin: *Dancing With Tears In My Eyes* • Milton Ager/Jack Yellen: *Big Boy* • Richard Rodgers/Lorenz Hart: *Thou Swell* • Harry Carroll/Joseph McCarthy: *I'm Always Chasing Rainbows* • Raymond Klages: *Sorry* • Harry B. Smith/Francis Wheeler/Ted Snyder: *The Sheik Of Araby* • Oscar Hammerstein II/Otto Harbach/Jerome Kern: *Who* • William Jerome/Jean Schwartz: *Chinatown, My Chinatown* • Sonny Miller: *Remember Me* • James P. Johnson/R.C. McPherson: *Charleston* • Ben Bernie/Kenneth Casey/Maceo Pinkard: *Sweet Georgia Brown* • Con Conrad/Gladys DuBois/Russ Colombo/Paul Gregory: *You Call It Madness (But I Call It Love)* • D. J. LaRocca/Larry Shields: *At The Jazz Band Ball* • Lew Brown/B.G. DeSylva/Ray Henderson: *It All Depends On You* • Fred E. Ahlert/Roy Turk: *I'll Get By*

2015

Irrational Man
(*Irrational Man*)
USA, ca. 96 Minuten

Regie: Woody Allen **Drehbuch:** Woody Allen **Produktion:** Letty Aronson/Stephen Tenenbaum/Edward Walson **Kamera:** Darius Khondji **Schnitt:** Alisa Lepselter **Kostüme:** Suzy Benzinger **Musik:** s. Musiktitel **Darsteller:** Joaquin Phoenix (*Abe*); Emma Stone (*Jill*); Parker Posey (*Rita*); Jamie Blackley (*Roy*); Sophie von Haselberg (*April*); Ben Rosenfield/Michael Goldsmith/Lindsey McWhorter/Meredith Hagner/Jamie Rosenstein (*Aprils Freunde*); Susan Pourfar (*Carol*); Gary Wilmes/David Aaron Baker/Nancy Villone (*Carols Freunde*); Joe Stapleton/Nancy Carroll (*Professoren*); Allison Gallerani/Brigette Lundy-Paine/Katelyn Semer (*Braylin Studenten*); Ethan Phillips (*Jills Vater*); Betsy Aidem (*Jills Mutter*); Leah Anderson (*Studentin, die Weg beschreibt*); Paula Plum (*College-Präsidentin*); Nancy Giles (*Assistentin der College-Präsidentin*); Henry Stram/Geoff Schuppert (*Cocktail-Party-Gäste*); Robert Petkoff (*Paul*); Alex Dunn (*Student im Seminarraum*); Ron Chez/Tamara Hickey (*Professoren in der Cafeteria*); Christine Mascott (*Kellnerin*); Tom Kemp (*Judge Spangler*); Britt Faulkner (*Studentin im Seminarraum*); Marina Re (*Kirmesangestellte*); David Pittu (*Professor bei der Fakultätssitzung*); Mark Zeisler (*TV-Ansager*); Adrienne Taylor (*Cellistin*); Tina Benko (*TV-Ansagerin*); Kate McGonigle (*Ellie*) Ungenannt: Amanda Blattner (*Professorin*); Ben Bocko (*Student*); David Boston (*Passant im Park*); Kaitlyn Bouchard (*Studentin*); Mark Burzenski (*Mann, der die Straße überquert*); Ana Marie Calise (*Studentin*); Terry Conforti (*Fakultätsmitglied*); Hannah Coppolelli (*Mädchen auf der Kirmes*); Jonah Coppolelli (*Junge auf der Kirmes*); Julie Ann Dawson (*Studentin*); Ariana DeFusco (*Studentin*); Curtis Eames (*Barkeeper*); Kate Flanagan (*Becky*); Jared M. Gordon (*Bridge-Club-Servierer*); Elaine Victoria Grey (*Mutter mit Sohn im Café/Nachbarin*); London Hall (*Professorin*); Abby Rain Heiser (*Mädchen auf auf der Kirmes*); Rosemary Howard (*Fußgängerin vor dem Café*); Steven Howitt (*Barbesucher*); Jessica Kent (*Studentin*); Jeffery Kincannon (*Fahrer*); Bryce Kipp (*Student*); Lauren Laperriere (*Studentin/Barbesucherin*); Christopher Lemieux (*Student*); Phyllis Lynn (*Professorin*); Allie Marshall (*Mädchen mit rotem Shirt auf der Party*); Margaret Maurer (*Studentin*); Marely Mercedes (*Studentin*); Randy Morris (*Dad*); Michaelah Noelle Nunes (*Mädchen auf der Kirmes*); Grady Oberton (*Junge auf der Kirmes*); Josette Oberton (*Mädchen auf der Kirmes*); Joseph Oliveira (*Mann auf dem Spielplatz*); Aaron Olson (*Student*); Rosemary Pacheco (*Spaziergängerin im Park*); Chris Palermo (*Cocktail-Party-Professor*); Gianni Paolo (*Kirmesbesucher*); Jon Perroni (*Partybesucher*); Haley Pine (*Mädchen auf der Kirmes*); Robert Popa (*Professor*); Gary Roscoe (*Fakultätsmitglied*); Halie Sabatasso (*Studentin*); Eva Senerchia (*Mädchen auf der Kirmes*); Dora Sexton (*Kinobesucherin*); Nancy Ellen Shore (*Fakultätsmitglied*); Jhennah Sinclaire (*Kellnerin*); David Struffolino (*Schaufenstergucker*); Michael Steven Swanson (*Professor*); Lino Tanaka (*Parkbesucher*); Carl „CJ" Tempesta (*Philosophiestudent*); Greg Terzis (*Student*); J. P. Valenti (*Kellner*); George Vezina (*Professor*); Pamela Figueiredo Wilcox (*Studentin*); Lisa Wynn (*Professorin*)[8]

Handlung: Ein renommierter Philosophieprofessor auf der Suche nach dem Sinn des Lebens: Abe Lucas befindet sich in einer existenziellen Krise. Er wechselt an eine Kleinstadtuniversität, wo er sich schon bald auf die Annäherungsversuche seiner Kollegin Rita einlässt und gleichzeitig eine zunächst nur platonische Freundschaft zu der jungen Studentin Jill unterhält. Bei einem Cafébesuch mit Jill wird er zufällig Zeuge eines Gesprächs am Nachbartisch. Danach ist Abe nicht mehr derselbe, seine Probleme scheinen sich in Luft aufgelöst zu haben. Doch den Menschen in seiner Umgebung ist diese Verwandlung irgendwann nicht mehr ganz geheuer…

---

[8] Informationen zur Besetzung aus: http://www.imdb.com/title/tt3715320/?ref_=nv_sr_1, Stand 15.09.2015

Musiktitel: : Billy Page: *The 'In' Crowd* • Daniel May: *Good To Go* • Michael Ballou: *Almathea; Cut Loose Mix II* • Ramsey E. Lewis: *Look-A-Here; Wade In The Water* • Johann Sebastian Bach: *Präludium und Fuge Nr. 2 c*-Moll BWV 847, aus dem *Wohltemperierten Klavier; Präludium und Fuge Nr. 18 gis*-Moll BWV 863, aus dem *Wohltemperierten Klavier; Cellosuite Nr. 1 für Violoncello Solo G*-Dur BWV 1007, 1. Präludium • Leo Friedmann/Beth Slater Whitson: *Let Me Call You Sweetheart* • Juventino Rosas: *Over The Waves* • Eddie DeLange/Jimmy Van Heusen: *Darn That Dream* • David O'Neal: *Angel In The Snow*[9]

Der Film wurde zum ersten Mal am 15.05.2015 beim Filmfestival in Cannes gezeigt. Kinostart in den USA: 17.07.2015/Kinostart in Deutschland: 12.11.2015[10]

---

[9] Informationen zum Soundtrack aus: http://www.soundtrack.net/movie/irrational-man/, Stand 15.09.2015
[10] Informationen aus: http://www.imdb.com/title/tt3715320/releaseinfo?ref_=tt_ql_9 und http://www.moviepilot.de/movies/irrational-man, jeweils Stand 15.09.2015

II. Die Filme – alphabetisch: Titel der deutschen Fassung

Alice	1990	Mach's Noch Einmal, Sam	1972
Alle Sagen: I Love You	1996	Magic In The Moonlight	2014
Antz	1998	Manhattan	1979
Anything Else	2003	Manhattan Murder Mystery	1993
Bananas	1971	Match Point	2005
Blue Jasmine	2013	Melinda Und Melinda	2004
Broadway Danny Rose	1984	Midnight In Paris	2011
Bullets Over Broadway	1994	New Yorker Geschichten	1989
Casino Royale	1967	Paris-Manhattan	2012
Cassandras Traum	2007	Plötzlich Gigolo	2013
Celebrity – Schön, Reich Und Berühmt	1998	Radio Days	1987
Der Schläfer	1973	Schatten Und Nebel	1991
Der Stadtneurotiker	1977	Schmalspurganoven	2000
Der Strohmann	1976	Scoop – Der Knüller	2000
Die Letzte Nacht Des Boris Gruschenko	1975	September	1987
Ehemänner Und Ehefrauen	1992	Sonny Boys – Zwei Wie Pech Und Schwefel	1996
Ein Ganz Normaler Hochzeitstag	1991	Stardust Memories	1980
Eine Andere Frau	1988	Sweet And Lowdown	1999
Eine Sommernachts-Sex-Komödie	1982	The Purple Rose Of Cairo	1985
Geliebte Aphrodite	1995	To Rome With Love	2012
Hannah Und Ihre Schwestern	1986	Verbrechen Und Andere Kleinigkeiten	1989
Harry Außer Sich	1997	Vicky Christina Barcelona	2008
Hollywood Ending	2002	Was Gibt's Neues, Pussy?	1965
Ich Hab Doch Nur Meine Frau Zerlegt	2000	Was Sie Schon Immer Über Sex Wissen Wollten …	1972
Ich Sehe Den Mann Deiner Träume	2010	Whatever Works – Liebe Sich Wer Kann	2009
Im Bann Des Jade Skorpions	2001	Whats's Up, Tiger Lily?	1966
Innenleben	1978	Woody, Der Unglücksrabe	1969
Irrational Man	2015	Zelig	1983
King Lear	1987		

III. Die Filme – alphabetisch: Titel der Originalfassung

A Midsummer Night's Sex Comedy	1982	**M**elinda And Melinda	2004
Alice	1990	**M**idnight In Paris	2011
Annie Hall	1977	**M**ighty Aphrodite	1995
Another Woman	1988	**N**ew York Stories	1989
Antz	1998	**P**aris-Manhattan	2012
Anything Else	2003	**Pi**cking Up The Pieces	2000
Bananas	1971	**P**lay It Again, Sam	1972
Blue Jasmine	2013	**R**adio Days	1987
Broadway Danny Rose	1984	**S**cenes From A Mall	1991
Bullets Over Broadway	1994	**S**coop	2006
Casino Royale	1967	**S**eptember	1987
Cassandra's Dream	2007	**S**hadows And Fog	1991
Celebrity	1998	**S**leeper	1973
Crimes And Misdemeanors	1989	**S**mall Time Crooks	2000
Deconstructing Harry	1997	**S**tardust Memories	1980
Everyone Says I Love You	1996	**S**weet And Lowdown	1999
Everything You Always Wanted To Know About Sex …	1972	**T**ake The Money And Run	1969
Fading Gigolo	2013	**T**he Curse Of The Jade Scorpion	2001
Hannah And Her Sisters	1986	**T**he Front	1976
Hollywood Ending	2002	**T**he Purple Rose Of Cairo	1985
Husbands And Wives	1992	**T**he Sunshine Boys	1996
Interiors	1978	**T**o Rome With Love	2012
Irrational Man	2015	**V**icky Christina Barcelona	2008
King Lear	1987	**W**hat's New Pussycat?	1965
Love And Death	1975	**W**hatever Works	2009
Magic In The Moonlight	2014	**W**hats's Up, Tiger Lily?	1966
Manhattan	1979	**Y**ou Will Meet A Tall Dark Stranger	2010
Manhattan Murder Mystery	1993	**Z**elig	1983
Match Point	2005		

IV. Musiktitel, die in mehreren Filmen gespielt werden

Musiktitel	Filmtitel
All The Things You Are *(Kern/Hammerstein II)*	*New York Stories (Oedipus Wrecks)* *Deconstructing Harry*
At The Jazz Band Ball *(LaRocca/Shields)*	*Bullets Over Broadway* *Magic In The Moonlight*
Avalon *(Rose/Jolson/DeSylva)*	*Hannah And Her Sisters* *Sweet And Lowdown*
Begin The Beguine *(Porter)*	*Broadway Danny Rose* *Radio Days*
Back To The Apple *(Foster/Basie)*	*Hannah And Her Sisters* *Paris-Manhattan*
Bewitched *(Rodgers/Hart)*	*Hannah And Her Sisters* *Paris-Manhattan*
Body And Soul *(Sour/Green/Eyton)*	*Stardust Memories* *Radio Days*
Caravan *(Ellington/Tizol/Mills)*	*Alice* *Sweet And Lowdown*
Cembalokonzert *f*-Moll BWV 1056 *(Bach)*	*Hannah And Her Sisters* *Paris-Manhattan*
Chinatown, My Chinatown *(Jerome/Schwartz)*	*Radio Days* *Everyone Says I Love You* *Magic In The Moonlight*
Cocktails For Two *(Coslow/Johnston)*	*Everyone Says I Love You* *Celebrity* *Small Time Crooks*
Crazy Rhythm *(Ceasar/Meyer/Kahn)*	*Crimes And Misdemeanors* *Bullets Over Broadway*
Darn That Dream *(DeLange/Van Heusen)*	*Alice* *Melinda And Melinda* *Irrational Man*
Die Moritat Von Mackie Messer *(Weill/Brecht)*	*Alice* *Shadows And Fog* *Magic In The Moonlight*
Easy To Love *(Porter)*	*Stardust Memories* *Scenes From A Mall* *Anything Else*
Eine Nacht Auf Dem Kahlen Berg *(Mussorgski)*	*Stardust Memories* *Deconstructing Harry*
Fascination *(Marchetti/Manning)*	*Celebrity* *Small Time Crooks*
Happy Birthday To You *(Hill/Hill)*	*Crimes And Misdemeanors* *What Ever Works*
Hochzeitsmarsch *(Mendelssohn-Bartholdy)*	*A Midsummer Night's Sex Comedy* *Whatever Works*

Musiktitel	Filmtitel
I Can't Believe That You're In Love With Me *(Gaskill/McHugh)*	*Everyone Says I Love You* *Anything Else*
I Love My Baby, My Baby Loves Me *(Green/Warren)*	*Zelig* *Purple Rose Of Cairo*
I Remember You *(Mercer/Schertzinger)*	*Hannah And Her Sisters* *Alice*
I'll Be Seeing You *(Fain/Kahal)*	*New York Stories (Oedipus Wrecks)* *Crimes And Misdemeanors*
If I Had You *(Campbell/Connelly/Shapiro)*	*Hannah And Her Sisters* *Everyone Says I Love You* *You Will Meet A Tall Dark Stranger*
I'll Get By *Ahlert/Turk*	*Zelig* *Magic In The Moonlight*
I'll See You In My Dreams *(Kahn/Jones)*	*Stardust Memories* *Sweet And Low Down* *You Will Meet A Tall Dark Stranger*
I'm In Love Again *(Porter)*	*Hannah And Her Sisters* *Paris-Manhattan*
In A Persian Market *(Ketèlbey)*	*New York Stories (Oedipus Wrecks)* *The Curse Of The Jade Scorpion*
It Could Happen To You *(Burke/Van Heusen)*	*Hannah And Her Sisters* *New York Stories (Life Studies)* *Anything Else*
Just One Of Those Things *(Porter)*	*Stardust Memories* *Radio Days*
Just You, Just Me *(Klages/Greer)*	*Hannah And Her Sisters* *Everyone Says I Love You*
Let's Do It *(Porter)*	*Scenes From A Mall* *Midnight In Paris*
Let's Misbehave *(Porter)*	*Everything You Always Wanted To Know …* *Bullets Over Broadway*
Limehouse Blues *(Braham/Furber)*	*Alice* *Sweet And Lowdown*
Make Believe *(Kern/Hammerstein II)*	*Another Woman* *Bullets Over Broadway*
Makin' Whoopee *(Donaldson/Kahn)*	*Husbands And Wives* *Everyone Says I Love You*
Miami Beach Rumba *(Fields/Gamse/Camacho)*	*Deconstructing Harry* *Scoop*

Musiktitel	Filmtitel
Moonglow (*Hudson/Mills/DeLange*)	*September* *Alice* *Melinda And Melinda*
Nessun Dorma (Turandot) (*Puccini*)	*New York Stories (Life Studies; Oedipus Wrecks)* *To Rome With Love*
Night And Day (*Porter*)	*Radio Days* *September*
No Moon At All (*Mann/Evans*)	*Hollywood Ending* *Melinda And Melinda*
On A Slow Boat To China (*Loesser*)	*September* *Celebrity*
Out Of Nowhere (*Green/Heyman*)	*September* *Manhattan Murder Mystery* *Deconstructing Harry* *Sweet And Lowdown*
Parlez-Moi d'Amour (*Lenoir*)	*Sweet And Lowdown* *Midnight In Paris*
Polkadots And Moonbeams (*Burke/Van Heusen*)	*Hannah And Her Sisters* *Crimes And Misdemeanors*
Poor Butterfly (*Hubbell/Golden*)	*Bullets Over Broadway* *Hollywood Ending*
Recado (*António/Ferreira*)	*Scoop* *Midnight In Paris*
Rosalie (*Porter*)	*Crimes And Misdemeanors* *Deconstructing Harry*
Sinfonie Nr. 5 (Schicksals-Sinfonie) *c*-Moll op. 67 (*Beethoven*)	*Celebritiy* *Whatever Works*
Sing, Sing, Sing (*Prima*)	*New York Stories (Oedipus Wrecks)* *Manhattan Murder Mystery* *Deconstructing Harry*
Sweet Georgia Brown (*Bernier/Casey/Pinkard*)	*Sturdust Memories* *Crimes And Misdemeanors* *Sweet And Lowdown* *Magic In The Moonlight*
Take Five (*Desmond*)	*Manhattan Murder Mystery* *Mighty Aphrodite*
That Old Feeling (*Brown/Fain*)	*Radio Days* *Husbands And Wives* *Celebrity*

Musiktitel	Filmtitel
The Best Things In Life Are Free *(DeSylva/Brown/Henderson)*	*Manhattan Murder Mystery* *Melinda And Melinda*
The ‚In' Crowd *(Page)*	*Mighty Aphrodite* *Irrational Man*
The Way You Look Tonight *(Kern/Fields)*	*Hannah And Her Sisters* *Alice* *Deconstructing Harry* *Anything Else*
Thou Swell *(Rodgers/Hart)*	*Bullets Over Broadway* *Magic In The Moonlight*
What Is This Thing Called Love? *(Porter)*	*New York Stories (Life Studies)* *Husbands And Wives*
When Day Is Done *(Katscher/DeSylva)*	*September* *Shadows And Fog* *Sweet And Lowdown*
When The Red, Red Robin Comes Bob Bob Bobbin Along *(Woods)*	*Bullets Over Broadway* *Deconstructing Harry*
When Your Lover Has Gone *(Swan)*	*Mighty Aphrodite* *To Rome With Love*
Who *(Kern/Harbach/Hammerstein II)*	*September* *Bullets Over Broadway* *Magic In The Moonlight*
Will You Still Be Mine *(Dennis/Adair)*	*Alice* *Celebrity* *Melinda And Melinda*
You Do Something To Me *(Porter)*	*Scenes From A Mall* *Mighty Aphrodite* *Midnight In Paris* *Magic In The Moonlight*
You'd Be So Nice To Come Home To *(Porter)*	*Radio Days* *Another Woman*

V. Register der Darsteller (Haupt- und Nebendarsteller)

A

Aaron, Caroline 32, 33, 36, 42
Abascal, Natividad 13
Abelanski, Lionel 66
Abraham, F. Murray 39
Abzug, Bella 19
Acevedo, Kirk 41
Ackerman, Stanley 12, 13, 20
Adam, Marie-Christine 61
Adams, Polly 44
Adams, Stanley 14
Addison, Bernard 44
Addy, William 37, 39, 44, 46
Adet, Georges 16
Adler, Jerry 37
Adu, Frank 16
Affif, Ron 45
Aidem, Betsy 67
Aiello, Danny 17, 24, 26
Akers, Karen 24
Albanese, Antonio 62
Albeck, Andy 20
Albert, Jean-Jacques 61
Albrecht, Liz 20
Alda, Alan 32, 37, 40
Alden, Howard 50
Allan, Laurena 64
Allen, Gary 18
Allen, Karen 19
Allen, Woody 10, 11, 12, 13, 14, 15, 16, 17, 18, 19, 20,
   21, 22, 23, 25, 26, 28, 31, 32, 34, 35, 36, 37, 39, 40,
   41, 42, 43, 46, 48, 49, 50, 51, 52, 55, 61, 62, 65
Alley, Kirstie 42
Almendral, Ami 40
Almquist, Gregg 26
Alper, Gary 39
Alpert, Sherman 65
Alphonse, Ronald 66
Alt, Carol 62
Alterman, Glen 35
Altman, Abe 65
Alvarez, Maricel 62
Amamoto, Hideyo 10
Amato, Gaetano 62
Ambrose, Joe 46
Ameri, Christian 61
Amerling, Cecilia 23
Amos, Diane 64
Anderson, Axel 13
Anderson, James 12

Anderson, Leah 67
André, Lola 31
Andress, Ursula 10, 11
Andrews, Natasha 66
Anspach, Susan 15
Antell, Pete 32
Anthony, Bill 19, 20
Anthony, Eugene 24
Anthony, Lysette 36
Anzell, Hy 13, 18, 26, 32, 42
Appel, Peter 34, 41
Aquilino, Frank 38
Aragón, Angélica 49
Arango, José Rafael 35
Aranha, Ray 42
Arau, Alfonso 49
Arden, Nancy 32
Ardeshir, Sam 38
Ardisson, Edmond 16
Argentieri, Maurizio 62
Argo, Victor 32, 34
Arianda, Nina 60
Arkin, Anthony 51, 52
Arluck, Neal 44
Armiliato, Fabio 62
Armstrong, Alexander 54, 55
Arnold, Annette 42
Arnold, Tichina 35
Aronin, Michael 18
Aronson, Alexa 42
Arquette, Rosanna 30
Arturo, Lisa 38
Ashton-Griffiths, Roger 59
Atkine, Féodor 16
Atkins, Eileen 66
Attaway, Roy 33
Atwell, Hayley 56
Augier, Albert 16
August, Ron 36
Aumont, Michel 61
Avery, Brian 15
Axelrod, Jack 13
Axler, George 23
Aykroyd, Dan 43, 50
Azaria, Hank 44
Azito, Tony 20

B

Backhouse, Carolyn 55
Badalucco, Michael 23, 41, 65
Bagdassarian, Serge 60

Bagley, Lorri 44
Bain, Conrad 13
Baker, Becky Ann 44
Baker, David Aaron 53, 67
Baker, Dylan 44
Baker, Mary Linn 19
Baker, Ronald 66
Balaban, Bob 33, 42, 65
Baldwin, Alec 33, 62, 64
Baler, Laura 35
Balint, Eszter 34
Ballard, Alba 23
Balmaceda, Madeline 40
Balter, James 18
Balutin, Jacques 10
Bancroft, Anne 43
Banderas, Antonio 59
Bandey, Paul 66
Bandhu, Ved 18
Bang, Joy 15
Barbato, Olga 23
Barbour, Thomas 21
Barbuto, Julia 23
Barceló, Manel 57
Bardem, Javier 57
Bardock, Matt 56
Bareikis, Arija 53
Bargonetti, Steve 46
Bari, Jade 20
Barkan, Ari 65
Barnes, Wade 20, 24
Baron, Lynda 55, 59
Baron, Sandy 23
Barrault, Marie-Christine 20
Barre, Gabriel 20
Barrett, Amy Louise 33
Barry, Jack 14
Barry-Barry, Ron 35
Barrymore, Drew 40
Barsaco, Yves 16
Barth, Ed 13
Bartlett, Robin 32, 33
Barudin, Amanda 42
Basile, Joseph 65
Basler, Marianne 60
Bastedo, Alexandra 11
Bates, Kathy 34, 60
Bates, Paul 25
Bathurst, Robert 55
Battista, Lloyd 16
Bauer Chris 42
Bauer, Chris 46
Bauer, Grace 12
Bauerlein, Judy 42
Baxter, Tommie 40, 44

Bayeux, Carole 46, 50
Bayldon, Geoffrey 11
Beardsley, Alice 22
Beaulieu, Valérie 66
Beck, Jackson 12, 26
Beck, John 15
Beckenstein, Ray 50
Becker, Gerry 44
Bee, Samantha 58
Beggins, Francis 22
Begley Jr., Ed 58
Behar, Joy 37
Behn, Noel 20, 29
Bell, Geoff 55
Bell, Kernan 38
Bell, Ralph 22
Bellan, Joe 64
Belle, Delphina 65
Bellow, Saul 22
Belmondo, Jean-Paul 11
Ben Taleb, M'Barka 65
Benfield, John 56
Benguigui, Catherine 60
Benigni, Roberto 62
Benjamin, Richard 42
Benko, Tina 67
Bennett, Albert S. 24
Bennett, Roberta 26
Bentley, John 17
Berard, Jack 16
Beregi, Oscar 14
Berger, Anna 32
Berger, Belle 23, 26
Berger, Robert 22
Bergl, Emily 64
Bergman, Teddy 65
Bergmann, Martin S. 32
Berkley, Elizabeth 50
Berle, Milton 23
Berman, Andrew Mark 34
Berman, Paul 26
Bern, Mina 44
Bernardi, Herschel 17
Bernstein, Andrew 17
Bernstein, Bill 32
Bernstein, Jacob 17
Bernstein, Walter 18
Berrington, Elizabeth 55
Bertoni, Riccardo 18, 48
Bertrán, Lloll 57
Bertrand, Eva 16
Berwick, Arthur 44
Besserer, Rob 48
Bettelheim, Dr. Bruno 22
Bhasker, Sanjeev 55

Bibic, Vladimir 44
Biggs, Jason 52
Bindinger, Emily 40
Bird, Lauri 18
Birt, George 16
Bisset, Jacqueline 11
Black, Lewis 25
Black, Rachel 38
Black, Teri 48
Blackley, Jamie 67
Blackman, Ilene 36
Blair, Pamela 39
Blake, Sydney A. 24, 26
Blakiston, Caroline 55
Blanchard, Tammy 64
Blanchett, Cate 64
Bland, John Harrington 64
Blattner, Amanda 67
Bloch, Merv 32, 36
Bloch, Scotty 40, 42, 48
Blocher, Kent 39
Block, Oliver 26
Bloom, Claire 32, 39
Blum, Prof. John Morton 22
Blumhagen, Lothar 43
Bluthal, John 11
Boatman, Ross 56
Bocko, Ben 67
Bodrozic, Milo 56
Bogert, William 17
Bogosian, Eric 42
Bogue, Kevin 40
Bolster, Thomas L. 32, 34
Bolus, Michael 46
Bond, Sheila 23
Bonham Carter, Helena 39
Bonini, Fabio 62
Bonotto, Matteo 62
Boone, Steve 10
Bordo, Edwin 23, 24
Borowitz, Andy 53
Borowitz, Katherine 65
Bosco, Philip 29, 34, 42
Bosniak, Sloane 20
Boston, David 67
Bouchard, Kaitlyn 67
Bouchet, Barbara 11
Bourou-Rubinsztein, Thérèse 60
Bowan, Sybil 18
Boyden, Peter 44
Boyer, Charles 11
Boylan, Mary 18
Bracchitta, Jim 41
Braden, John 13
Bradley, Diane 48

Brady, Moya 55
Braff, Zach 37
Brainville, Yves 16
Branagh, Kenneth 44
Bremner, Ewen 54, 59
Brenner, Maurice 24
Bricktop 22
Bridges, Lynda 33
Britton, Burt 17
Briz 31
Broadbent, Jim 38
Brocksmith, Roy 20
Brodsky, Jack 35
Brody, Adrien 30, 60
Brolin, Josh 53, 59
Brooks, Adam 58
Brophy, Brian 49
Brous, Sharon 20
Brown, Benjamin Franklin 46
Brown, Bruce 50
Brown, Garrett 22
Brown, Michael 35
Bruce, Amanda 35
Bruel, Patrick 61
Bruni, Carla 60
Bruno, Jerry 42
Bruschetta, Ninni 62
Bryant, Al 46
Buache, Freddy 28
Bucher, John 36
Buck, Joe 42
Buck, Waltrudis 40, 42
Buckley, Betty 29
Buckwalter, John 22
Bud, Joan 31
Budin Jones, Terry 56
Buff, Sarah 44
Buhr, Gerard 16
Buntzen, Rob 53
Burdoe, Phyllis 42, 48
Burge, James 18
Burke, Marylouise 44
Burkhardt, Gerry 40
Burns, Stan 26
Burton, Kate 44
Burton, Richard 10
Burzenski, Mark 67
Buscemi, Steve 30
Bustamante, Augustin 35
Bustric, Sergio 62
Butler, Artie 26
Butler, Joe 10
Buttafuoco, Joey 44
Buttafuoco, Mary Joe 44
Byrne, Anne 19

C

C.K., Louis 64
Caban, Angel 44
Cadell, Selina 54
Cahoon, Kevin 50
Caillou, Alan 14
Caine, Michael 25
Calabrese, Josephine 48
Caldwell, Zoe 24
Cale, David 26
Calise, Ana Marie 67
Callahan, Lee 18
Callaway, William 18
Callinan, Dick 13
Calvani, Luca 62
Camerini, Duccio 62
Cammarano, Rita 62
Campbell, Erma 22
Canfield, Gene 38
Cannavale, Bobby 64
Cannon, Jack 22
Cantu, Martin 64
Canuel, Lindsy 40
Caparrini, Simona 62
Capriotti, Cecilia 62
Capucine 10
Cara, Ruggero 62
Caravella, Bobby 35
Carax, Léos 28
Carell, Steve 53
Carlin, Joy 64
Carmen 18, 23, 44, 50
Carr, Larry Robert 20
Carradine, John 14
Carrado, Jay 52
Carrey, Leah 26
Carroll, Barbara 51
Carroll, Beeson 13
Carroll, Nancy 67
Carrotte 25
Carson, Wayne 18
Carter, Dan 56
Carter, Jim 56
Carter, John 44
Carvalho, Betty 49
Carver, Cindy 48
Casella, Max 64, 65
Casey, Eileen 40
Casey, Shaun 18
Caspillo, Glen 64
Castellano, Donna 32
Castellotti, Peter 23, 24, 26, 38, 42, 44
Castillo, Enrique 49
Cavalicro, Rosie 55

Cavett, Dick 18
Cavill, Henry 58
Ceballos, René 39, 40
Cecere, Vinicio 62
Cecil, Jane 28
Cerullo, Al 39
Cervera Jr., Jorge 49
Chabanol, Loan 65
Chae, Sunny 42
Chaib, Elie 39
Chan, Kim 33
Channing, Stockard 52
Chapin, Ken 20, 22, 24
Chaplin, Geraldine 11
Chapman, Georgina 54
Chapman, Lonny 12
Chapman, Ted 13
Charone, Irwin 42
Châtelier, Margaux 61
Chatinover, Marvin 22, 31, 42, 48
Cheng, Barney 51
Cheng, Diana 33
Cherry, Alfred 33
Cherry, Vivian 40
Chez, Ron 67
Chiara, Maria 25
Childress, Yolanda 26
Chodorov, Samuel 20
Chomnalez, Pedro 66
Chuy, Don 14
Cimino, Leonardo 20
Ciron, Jacques 61
Cividanes, Robert 44
Claret, Laurent 60
Clark, Andrew 26
Clark, Dort 14
Clarke, Antonia 66
Clarke, David 17
Clarkson, Patricia 57, 58
Claudel, Aurélie 65
Clay, Andrew Dice 64
Clemenson, Christian 25
Clifton, Isaiah 65
Cobitt, Cindy 40
Coburn, Brian 16
Cohen, Alexander 24
Cohen, Gladys 61
Cohen, Judith 20
Cohen, Lynn 37, 42
Cohen, Ray 42, 44
Cole, Gardenia 20
Coleman, Joseph P. 39
Coles Sr., Marshall 22
Colicchio, Victor 38, 44
Collins, Nancy 19

Collins, Pauline 59
Colner, Marc 26
Colorado, Vira 35
Compton, O'Neal 49
Conaway, Cristi 36
Condé, Marie-Sohna 60
Conforti, Terry 67
Conforti, Tony 38
Conrad, David 52
Conrad, Marion 10
Conroy, Frances 19, 29, 32
Conti, Richard 64
Cooper, Elana 31
Cooper, Terence 11
Coppolelli, Hannah 67
Coppolelli, Jonah 67
Corbett, Ronnie 11
Cord, Elisabeth Anne 42
Cordier, Tom 60
Corey, Prof. Irwin 50
Cornwell, Phil 55
Correia, Don 40
Cortes, Vincent Menjou 60
Corti, Federica 62
Cortino, Anthony 33
Cosell, Howard 13, 23
Costelloe, John 37, 44
Costigan, Ken 25
Cotillard, Marion 60
Coué, Jérôme 61
Coutet, Henri 16
Cowen, Henry 26
Cox, Brian 54
Cragin, Charles 34, 38
Craig, Wendell 26
Craig, Windy 22
Cramer, Alison 38
Crane, Dagne 13
Cranshaw, Patrick 40
Craze, Galaxy 36
Crecco, Michael 44
Cribbins, Bernard 11
Crisp, Tracey 11
Crist, Judith 20
Crow, Thomas P. 32
Crowley, Ed 13
Crown, Patricia 16
Crudup, Billy 40
Cruz, Leonel 35
Cruz, Penélope 57, 62
Crystal, Billy 42
Cuccioli, Robert 44
Cucinotta, Maria Grazia 49
Cuervo, Alma 44
Cummings, Richard 40

Curtin, Jane 43
Cusack, John 34, 38
Cuthrell-Tuttleman, Willa 58
Czarniak, Henry 16

D

D'Amodio, Charles 23
D'Angelo, Beverly 18
D'Arbanville, Patti 44
Dahm, Gretchen 29
Daloise, Sean 44
Daly, Patrick 20
Daly, Peter Hugo 56
Dana, Al 40
Dance, Charles 55
Daniels, Jeff 24, 26
Danneberg, Thomas 43
Danner, Blythe 29, 33, 36
Danon, Denice 20
Dark, Peter 45
Darrow, Tony 38, 39, 42, 44, 46, 48
David, Joanna 59
David, Larry 26, 31, 58
Davidson, Jack 17
Davila, Diana 15
Davis, Eddy 46
Davis, Humphrey 18
Davis, Judy 33, 36, 42, 44, 62
Davis, Paul 56
Davis, Phil 56
Davis, Sylvia 20
Dawson, Julie Ann 67
Day, Matt 55
De Beer, Baron 13
de Benito, Emilio 57
de Fluiter, Stephen 25
De La Paz, Danny 49
De La Pena, George 39
De La Torre, Jeannine 49
de Lencquesaing, Louis-Do 61
De Lorenzo, Massimo 62
De Ruggieri, Carlo 62
De Van, Adrien 60
De Vita, Paolo 62
De Vito, Francesco 62
Deakin, Julia 55
Dean, E. Brian 20
DeAngelis, Gina 23, 26
DeBonis, Marcia 58
DeCheser, Allen 25
DeCheser, Artie 25
DeFusco, Ariana 67
Degidon, Tom 24
Deitch, Louise 22

Delaney, Joan 35
Delaney, Shelley 26
Delano, Laura 20
Dell Orefice, Carmen 44
Della Casa, Roberto 62
Delouya, Raphaël 61
Delpy, Julie 28
Delterme, Marine 61
Demay, Sally 20
Demian, Marcus 49
Denney, Charles 22
Dennis, Sandy 29
Dennis, Tom 20
Dentice, Keith 18
Derocker, Jeff 40
Derwin, Jordan 20
DeSalvo, Anne 20
DeSimone, Kevin 40
DeVito, Danny 52
Dewhurst, Colleen 18
Di Brigida, Rosa 62
Di Fonzo Bo, Marcial 60
Di Rauso, Margherita 62
Diamantidou, Despo 16
Diamond, Val 64
DiBenedetto, John 38
DiCaprio, Leonardo 44
Dick, Andy 49
Dickson, Clifford Lee 58
Dierlam, Katy 34
DiMauro, Joanne 39
Dixon, Jade 65
Dixon, McIntyre 17
Dolezar, Gerald E. 38
Domènech, Josep Maria 57
Don, Carl 20
Donald, Juliana 24
Dorian, Bob 50, 51
Doumanian, John 18, 19, 20, 22, 23, 25, 36, 37, 38, 42, 44, 48, 50
Dowis, Bernice 22
Doyle, Kathleen 39, 44
Draeger, Wolfgang 43
Drescher, Fran 49
Dudley, Robert 13
Duffy, Karen 44
Duffy, Kerry 19
Dugan Slater, Doris 20
Dukakis, Olympia 39
Dummont, Denise 26
Duncan, Ben 46
Dunk, Jim 55
Dunn, Alex 67
Dunn, Colleen 40
Dunn, Kevin 57
Dunphy, Don 13
Dunst, Kirsten 31
Durkin, Thomas 39
Durning, Michele 53
Duvall, Shelley 18

E

Eames, Curtis 67
Ecklund, Peter 50
Edelman, Gregg 32, 51
Edelson, Kenneth 33, 36, 39, 42, 44, 46, 48, 50, 51, 52, 53, 56, 58, 60, 64, 66
Edson, Richard 49
Edwards, Annie-Joe 24, 31, 38
Egz, Lexi 46
Ehrenreich, Alden 64
Eidelsberg, Joel 26, 51
Eisenberg, Jesse 62
Eisenberg, Ned 44
Ejiofor, Chiwetel 53
Eles, Sandor 16
Elli 65
Elliott, Denholm 28
Elmaleh, Gad 60
Emilfork, Daniel 10
Eng, Melinda 44
Ennasri, Khereddine 61
Enríquez, René 13
Ephron, Nora 32, 36
Eppolito, Lou 38
Erskine, Drummond 46
Erskine, Howard 22, 38, 44, 48, 50, 51
Erwin, Lee 26
Esposito, Giovanni 62
Esposito, Jennifer 41
Evans, Norman 13
Evans, Paul 40
Everett, Pamela 40
Ewert, Carola 43

F

Fabiole, Luce 16
Fadda, Giacomo 62
Faith, Chrissy 40
Falco, Edie 38, 41
Falk, Peter 41
Falkowski, Hilma 65
Fallon, Jimmy 52
Faragallah, Ramsey 44, 48, 50, 51
Farina, Michael J. 53
Farrell, Colin 56
Farrell, Tom Riis 34
Farrelly, Patrick 35

Farrow Previn, Fletcher 25, 26
Farrow, Mia 21, 22, 23, 24, 25, 26, 28, 29, 31, 32, 33, 34, 36
Farrow, Moses 25
Farrow, Stephanie 22, 24
Farrow, Tisa 19
Farwood, Dean 64
Faulkner, Britt 67
Faye, Denise 39
Faye, Joey 17
Fedotowsky, Ali 64
Feldman, Lawrence 50
Ferland, Danielle 26, 39
Ferrell, Will 53
Ferrer, José 21
Ferrol, Sharon 22
Ferroni, Massimo 62
Field, Crystal 24, 26, 48
Field, Todd 26
Fierstein, Harvey 38
Filali, Marianne 39
Fink, Dann 39
Fink, Randy Aaron 32
Finkel, Barry 32
Finn, Shannon 64
Finocchiaro, Donatella 62
Firestone, Daren 35
Firth, Colin 66
Fisher, Carrie 25
Fisher, Tom 56
Fishman, Larry 20
Fitzgerald, Donegal 44
Flanagan, Kate 67
Flanagan, William 26
Fleming, Erin 14
Fleshler, Glenn 64
Fletcher, Mari 15
Fleurot, Audrey 60
Flint, Matthew 36
Flippin, Lucy Lee 17, 18
Florian 16
Fogel, Joel S. 32
Fogt, Jacqueline 10, 16
Folk, Abel 57
Forbes, Chris 15
Ford, Clebert 44
Forde, Jessica 66
Fornari, Augusto 62
Forsythe, Henderson 19
Forte, Nick Apollo 23
Fortuna, Corrado 62
Fortune, John 54
Foster, Jodie 34
Fowler, Cate 56
Fowler, Monique 44

Fowler, Scott 39
Fox, Dorothi 13
Fraboni, Angelo 39
Frank, Janet 29
Frankel, Shelley 40
Franklin, Joe 23
Frankston, Jessica 36
Frazer, Dan 12, 13, 42
Frazer, Rupert 55, 59
Freeman, Ann 20
French, Adele 31
French, Jacqueline 20
Frieder, Sol 16, 21, 32, 65
Friedman, Bruce Jay 29, 36, 44
Friedman, Daniel 20
Friedman, Dee Dee 29
Friedman, Lisa 20
Friedman, Robert 20
Friel, Anna 59
Friend, Sam 55
Frigerio, Gustavo 62
Frost, Jean Sarah 18
Frye, David 35
Fulford, Christopher 55, 59
Fuller, Kurt 60

G

Gabriel, Peter 30
Gale, Edra 10
Gallagher Jr., John 58
Gallagher, Gina 33
Gallerani, Allison 67
Gallo, Barbara 26
Gallo, Joie 23
Gampel, Chris 18
Garai, Romola 55
Gardner, Paul 56
Garfield, Allen 13
Garfield, Julie 17
Garfinkle, Nick 48
Garner, Jennifer 42
Garrett, Brad 46
Garrett, Robert 35
Garrick, Barbara 64
Garrison, Ellen 22
Garvey, Ray 39, 40, 42, 46, 48, 50, 51, 52
Gaston, Penny 19, 35
Gatiss, Mark 54
Gay, Caroline 61
Gayle, Jackie 23
Gayton, Clark 46
Gecks, Eleanor 59
Gelber, Jack 29
Gelfman-Randazzo, Juliet 42

Geller, Marc 20
Gemma, Giuliano 62
Gennaro, Gino 17
Georges-Picot, Olga 16
Gerard, Greg 26
Gerber, Bill 44, 48, 51
Gerety, Peter 50, 51
Gertsacov, Seth 39
Gerwig, Greta 62
Gescher, Norbert 43
Getz, Ileen 44
Gewertz, Perry 20
Giamatti, Paul 39, 42
Giannini, Giancarlo 30
Gibb, Cindy 20
Gibson, Rebecca 34
Giftos, Elaine 14
Gilchrist, Emily 54, 56
Giles III, Brooks 46
Giles, Nancy 31, 67
Ginsburg, Susan 20
Gioiello, Bruno 44
Giordano, Jonathan 40
Giordano, Vince 46, 50
Girard, Wendy 18
Gleason, Joanna 25, 32
Glenister, Philip 59
Glenn, Rebecca 36
Glover, Danny 43
Glover, John 18
Glover, Julian 55
Godard, Jean-Luc 28
Godwin, Christopher 55
Goehner, Fred 46
Gold, Judy 50
Goldberg, Whoopi 41
Goldblum, Jeff 18
Golden, Heather 35
Goldner, Judy 20
Goldsmith, Merwin 41
Goldsmith, Michael 67
Goldstein, Michael 20
Gondard, Paul-Edouard 61
Goode, Matthew 54
Goodman, Hazelle 42
Gordon, Colin 11
Gordon, Jared M. 67
Gordon, Mark 12
Gordon-Clark, Susan 25
Gordon-Levitt, Joseph 49
Gorgone, Nusia 62
Gorruso, Anthony 32
Gottschall, Ruth 40
Gough, Lloyd 17
Gouix, Guillaume 60

Gould, Elliott 49
Gould, Eric 18
Gould, Gordon 22
Gould, Harold 16
Grace, Darius 49
Graham, Billy 35
Graham, Joseph G. 24
Graham, Richard 56
Grant, Hugh 48
Grant, Sean 40
Graves, Kristy 33
Gray, Diva 40
Gray, Sam 44
Greco, Paul 23
Green, Colton 40
Green, Seth 26
Greenberg, Jerry Tov 20
Greene, Michael 15, 35
Greenhill, Amy 25
Greenhouse, Martha 13
Greenhut, Jennifer 39
Gregory, Andre 44
Gregory, Mary 15
Grenier, Adrian 44, 52
Gressmann, Evelyn 43
Grey, Elaine Victoria 67
Griffin, Eddie 49
Griffin, John 40
Griffith, Kristin 19
Griffith, Melanie 44
Grimsby, Roger 13
Grizzard, George 48
Grody, Kathryn 29
Grollman, Elaine 24
Groninger, Kelly 38
Grossman, Edith 20
Grund, Richard 31
Guanciale, Lino 62
Guastaferro, Vincent 46
Guerra, Jackie 49
Guisset, Roman 61
Gunty, Morty 23
Guss, Jonathan 35
Gustin, Lisa 36
Gwynne, Fred 34

H

Haas, Lukas 40
Haber, Daniel 25
Hack, Shelley 18
Hackman, Gene 29, 43
Haddon, Dayle 38, 44
Hagan, Kevin 40
Hagerty, Julie 21

Hagner, Meredith 67
Hahn, Jess 10
Haidorfer, Karin 39
Hale, Helen 20
Hale, Victoria 42
Hall, London 67
Hall, Rebecca 57
Halley Jr., Major 32
Halse, Jody 55
Halston, Julie 39, 44, 48
Hama, Mie 10
Hamill, Katie 46
Hamilton, George 51
Hamilton, Josh 29
Hamilton, Victoria 55
Hamlin, George 22, 24
Hammer, Roger 26
Hammond, Mark 24
Hancisse, Thierry 60
Handy, Scott 54
Hanft, Helen 19, 20, 24, 31
Hankin, Harry 16
Hannah, Daryl 32
Hanover, Donna 44
Hansen, Gale 22
Harden, Marcia Gay 66
Hardwick, Mark 23
Hardy, Françoise 10
Harlow, Shalom 53
Harm, Michael 56
Harper, Jessica 16, 20
Harper, Phil 30
Harper, Robert 42
Harris, Carol 35
Harris, Johnny 59
Harris, Viola 42
Harris, Wood 44
Harrison, Kelly 59
Hart, Kitty Carlisle 26
Harter, James 20
Hawkins, Sally 56, 64
Hawkins, Yvette 39
Hawn, Goldie 40
Hayden, Pam 35
Hayes, Devalle 40
Hayes, Lortensia 42
Hayes, Roland 40
Hayman, Olivia 40, 48, 51
Haymer, Johnny 18
Head, Anthony 55
Headley, Glenne 24
Heap, Mark 55
Hecht, Jessica 58
Heck, Yves 60
Hedahl, Mary 24

Hegarty, Mary 54
Heiser, Abby Rain 67
Helleny, Joel 50
Hellman, Bonnie 20
Hemingway, Mariel 19, 42
Hengst, Marilyn 13
Henry, Alexi 33
Hentoff, Net 46
Hepner, Daniel 64
Herbert, Percy 11
Herlihy, Ed 22
Herlin, Jacques 61
Herman, Paul 24, 26, 31, 38, 39
Hernandez, Telmo 35
Herold, Bernie 22
Herrmann, Edward 24
Hershey, Barbara 25
Hibbert, Edward 40
Hickey, Tamara 67
Hiddleston, Tom 60
Higgins, Clare 56
Higgins, Michael 21
Higham, Jennifer 56
Hill, Conleth 58
Hill, William 41, 48, 52
Hillaire, Marcel 12
Hirsch, Selma 31
Hirt, Eléonore 10
Hoagland, Dante 65
Hobbs, Peter 15
Hodson, Ed 40
Hoffman, Jane 42
Hoffmann, Gaby 40
Holasek, Vanina 20
Holden, William 11
Holder, Geoffrey 14
Hollander, Barbara 40, 42
Hollander, Jack 20
Holm, Ian 29
Holmes, Rick Vincent 53
Holt, Toni 14
Holt, Will 22
Hope, Missy 19
Hopkins, Anthony 59
Horgan, Patrick 22, 50
Horne, J. R. 26
Horovitch, David 56
Horton, Russell 18
House, Henry 20
Houseman, John 29
Howard, Andrew 56
Howard, David S. 32, 42
Howard, Rosemary 67
Howe, Irving 22
Howitt, Steven 67

Hoyland, William 55
Hsu, Emily 64
Huertas, Jon 49
Huff, Neal 51
Hughes, Arthur 13
Hugot, Marceline 33
Hunt, Helen 50
Hurt, Mary Beth 19
Hurt, William 33
Hurwitz, Steve 51
Hussong, Will 22
Huston, Anjelica 11, 32, 37
Huston, John 11
Hutchings, Geoffrey 59
Hyde, Jacquelyn 12
Hyman, Dick 50

I

Iacona, Richard 45
Iacono, Lucy 23
Iacovino, Nick 38
Iglesia, Robert 22
Imrie, Celia 59
Ireland, Douglas 20
Irizarry, Gloria 37
Irving, Amy 42
Irwin, Bill 35
Ivey, Dana 29
Ivey, Lela 24

J

Jackman, Hugh 55
Jackson, Jeanine 22
Jackson, Neil 59
Jackson, Reuben 44
Jacobi, Amanda 51
Jacobi, Lou 14
Jacobson, Nate 12
Jacobson, Peter 42
Jahier, Donna Sue 64, 65
James, Sondra 39
James, Theo 59
Jamrog, Joe 17
Janney, Allison 44
Janssen, Famke 44
Jarchow, Bruce 26
Jarvis, Jane 26
Jasper, Zina 32
Jay, Tony 16
Jenkins, Richard 25
Jenkins, Thimothy 21
Jenks, Daniel 64
Jerome, Timothy 36, 40, 42, 44

Jerosa, Vincent 22
Jeter, Michael 22
Jewkowsky, Sid 42
Jiang, Yi-Wen 53
Joan, Joel 57
Johansson, Scarlett 54, 55, 57
John, Tommy 40
Johnson, Deborah 20
Johnson, Georgann 17
Johnson, Marc Damon 46
Johnson, Petronia 18
Johnson, Richard 55
Johnson, Van 24
Johnston, John Dennis 18
Jones, Cherylyn 40
Jones, Christine 18
Jones, Gemma 59
Jones, Ron Cephas 46
Jong, Erica 44
Jordan, Randy 45
Jordan, Richard 19
Jordan, Will 23
Joseph, Aubrey 65
Josepher, Sam 48
Joy, Robert 26, 34

K

Kah, Ariana 61
Kamarr 35
Kamarr, Kathy 35
Kane, Carol 18
Kanouse, Lyle 58
Karen, Nicole 10
Karm, Michael 18
Karr, Patti 39
Kasznar, Kurt 11
Kauders, Sylvia 32, 37
Kavner, Julie 25, 26, 31, 33, 34, 42
Kaye, Paul 54
Keane, James 30
Keaton, Diane 15, 16, 18, 19, 26, 37
Kebbell, Toby 54
Keefer, Don 15
Keegan, Rose 54
Kelber, Donnie 35
Kelif, Atmen 60
Kell, Michael 22, 44
Kellicutt, Conor 64
Kellin, Orange 46
Kelly, Janis 54
Kemp, Emme 46
Kemp, Tom 64, 67
Kennedy, Mimi 60
Kennedy, Tracy 25

Kent, Jessica 67
Keosian, Jessie 31
Kerr, Deborah 11
Kerr, Robin 55
Keto, Kelly 66
Kewer, Suzy 55
Keyes, Irwin 20
Keyser, Sunny 32
Khakh, Robert 40
Khan, Shaheen 59
Kher, Anupam 59
Khosla, Surinder 44
Kiani, Mohammid Nabi 20
Kieserman, David 23, 24
Kimbrough, Charles 17
Kincannon, Jeffery 67
Kinney, Kathy 49
Kipp, Bryce 67
Kirby, Michael 29, 34
Kirchmer, Tom 45
Kirk, Christina 53
Kissel, Howard 20
Kissell, David 23
Klein, Gerald 22
Klein, I.W. 17
Klein, Trude 40, 50
Kluckert, Jürgen 43
Knepper, Robert 40
Koch, Mayor Edward I. 31
Korzen, Anne 20
Kotkin, Edward S. 20, 26
Krall, Diana 52
Kramer, David H. 39
Krause, Rudolf 66
Krauss, Helmut 43
Kreisler, Katie 53
Krell, Ness 65
Kroft, Steve 48
Kronenfeld, Ivan 25, 26
Kruh, Juliette 61
Krupa, Olek 58
Kubiak, Thomas 24
Kuchma, Anna 65
Kuehn, Jurgen 22
Kulish, Kyle 44
Kullman, Wynter 52
Kunz, Simon 54
Kurland, Jeffrey 36, 39
Kurnitz, Julie 26
Kurobe, Susumu 10
Kuzmina, Eugenia 65

L

La Lumia, Drinda 24
Lacy, Jerry 15
Lakhdar, Mohamed 61
Lamberts, Jennifer 38
Landau, Martin 32
Landers, Alan 18
Lane, Ed 22
Lane, Marie 20
Lange, Anne 34
Lanza, Suzanne 28
Lanzano, Richard 23
Lanzoni, Fabio 35
LaPaglia, Anthony 46
LaPaglia, Jonathan 42
Laperriere, Lauren 67
Laredo, Ruth 48
Laslo, Mary 29
Lasser, Louise 10, 12, 13, 14, 20
Last, Ruth 37, 51
Laumeister, Shannah 38
Lavery, Patrick 40
Lavi, Daliah 11
Lawner, Mordecai 18
Lawrence, Amanda 59
Le Bow, Guy 26
Leavitt, Max 20
Lee, China 10
Lee, Darren 40
Leerhsen, Erica 51, 52, 66
Leff, Henry 12
Leffert, Joel 42
Legardy, Wanakee 35
LeGuillou, Lisa 40
Leighton, Bernie 25, 29
Lemieux, Christopher 67
Lemkow, Tutte 16
Lemper, Ute 66
Lenard, Mark 18
Lenkowsky, Philip 20
Lenoir, Jack 16
Lensky, Leib 16
Leo, Edoardo 62
Leon, Dorothy 20
Leoni, Téa 51
Lerer, Shifra 42
Lerner, Michael 44
Lescurat, François 61
Leung, Peter 46
Levi, Irit 64
Levin, Charles 18, 19
Levins, Maureen P. 20
Levinsky, Ken 26
Levinsky, Walter 32
Levitan, Amy 18
Levy, Jacques 29
Levy, Jesse 48

Levy, Lawrence 48
Levy, Philip 36, 37, 50
Lewis, Juliette 36
Lewis, Robert Q. 14
Lewkowicz, Chuck 46
Li, Honggang 53
Li, Weigang 53
Lichterman, Marvin 17
Licudi, Gabriella 11
Lieu, Fran 65
Light, John 55
Linari, Peter 50
Lindsay, Nigel 55
Linklater, Hamish 66
Lintern, Richard 56
Lipman, David 20, 41
Lippin, Renée 20, 26, 44
Lisa Marie 33
Litt, Richard 22
Lloyd, Eric 42
Locarro, Joe 40
Lochart, Ann 35
Lolov, Sava 60
Lombard, Peter 26
Lomita, Sol 20, 22
Long, Andrew 64
Long, Jodi 31, 33, 44
Longwell, Karen 39
Lonnberg, Anne 16
Loomis, Tim 34
Lopert, Tanya 10
Lopez, Jennifer 43
Loud, Sherman 22
Louis-Dreyfus, Julia 25, 42
Lovelle, Herb 50
Loveman, Leonore 32
Loving, Candy 20
Lovitz, Jon 48
Lowe, Charles 20
Lowe, David 60
Loy, Mary 61
Ludlam, Helen 18
Ludwig, Karen 19
Luke, Keye 33
Lumet, Baruch 14
Lumont, Roger 16
Lund, Julie 48
Lundh, Daniel 60
Lundy-Paine, Brigette 67
Lutter III, Alfred 16
Lyles, Leslie 64
Lynch, James 24
Lynn, Phyllis 67
Lyonne, Natasha 40
Lyons, Jeff 40

M

Maccone, Ronald 23
Machado, Manuella 20
Mack, Tom 14
Mack, Tommy 56
MacLane, Gretchen 24
MacMilian, Andrew 31
MacNeal, Catherine 64
Macpherson, Elle 33
Macqueen, Alex 59
Macrae, Duncan 11
MacRae, Heather 14
Macy, W. H. 26, 34
Madekwe, Ashley 56
Madonna 34
Maestro, Mía 49
Magee, Rusty 25
Magerman, William 26
Maguire, Tobey 42
Mahoney, John 43
Maidment, Steve 32
Mailer, Kate 28
Mailer, Norman 28
Mailer, Stephen 29
Malina, Judith 26
Malinowski, Chester 32
Malkovich, John 34
Mangiante, Alberto 62
Manishor, Michael 42
Mann III, Fred 39, 40
Mannain, Brian 26
Manos, George 24, 32, 33, 37
Mansfield, Philip 54
Mantegna, Joe 33, 44
Mantle, Doreen 55
Mantz, Delphine T. 40
Marchevet, Olivier 66
Marchia, Ray 26
Marchioni, Vinicio 62
Marchionne, Pierluigi 62
Marco, Anton 22
Marcovicci, Andrea 17
Marcus, Dominic 39
Marcus, Ed 16
Margolin, Janet 12, 18
Margulies, David 17, 44, 65
Marin, Cheech 49
Mark, Michael 40
Markell, Jodie 51
Markinson, Brian 46, 48, 50
Markland, Ted 15
Marlow, Janet 44, 45
Marni, Heather 44
Maroff, Bob 18, 20

Mars, Kenneth 26, 34
Marsais, David 61
Marshall, Allie 67
Marshall, E. G. 19
Martel, Julie 61
Martin Martell, Arlene 40
Martin, George 24
Martin, Ivan 51
Marx, Margaret 29
Mas, Miguel 49
Mascott, Christine 67
Mashimo, Fritz 49
Mason, Anthony 44
Mason, Darrell 35
Mason, Pamela 14
Masso, George 32
Mastin, Peter 55
Mastrin, Carmin 20
Mastronardi, Alessandra 62
Matteo, Dom 23
Matteucci, Brunella 62
Maurel-Sithole, Linda 40
Maurer, Margaret 67
Maury, Jacques 16
Mawe, Richard 44, 48
Maxwell, Wayne 20
May, Elaine 48
Mazar, Debi 38
Mazursky, Betsy 35
Mazursky, Paul 35, 43
Mazzola, Jeff 38, 42, 44, 51
McAdams, Rachel 60
McCarthy, Maggie 56
McCarthy, Patrick 44
McCloud, Damon 40
McComb, Heather 30
McComb, Jennifer Lynn 29
McConnachie, Brian 36, 38, 42, 44, 48, 50
McCormack, Brian 45
McCormack, Catherine 66
McCormick, Carolyn 58
McDaniel, James 33
McDonough, Kit 49
McGee, Caroline 29
McGee, Fran 38
McGonigle, Kate 67
McGrath, Douglas 44, 46, 48, 51
McGregor, Ewan 56
McGregor-Stewart, Kate 21
McHugh, Joanne 40
McIntyre, Earl P. 46
McKay, Christian 59
McKay, Scott 17
McKean, Michael 41, 58
McKinley, Narcissa 16

McKrell, Jim 18
McLarty, Zach 52
McLaughlin, John P. 46
McLaurine, Marcus 46
McLiam, John 15
McLuhan, Marshall 18
McMurray, Sam 17
McNally, Kevin R. 55
McNamara, Annie 64
McNamara, Maureen 44
McNamara, Patrick 17
McPhillips, Edward 22
McQuaid, Jimmy 39
McRobbie, Peter 22, 24, 34, 38, 39, 42, 44, 48
McShane, Ian 55
McSwain, Monica 40
McWhorter, Lindsey 67
Meadows, Carol Lee 38
Meer, Alicia 42, 44
Melamed, Fred 25, 26, 29, 32, 34, 36, 51
Mellinger, Susan 18
Mellor, Steve 44
Mercedes, Marely 67
Mercedes, Yvette 46
Meredith, Burgess 28
Merediz, Olga 41
Merlin, Jan 12
Messina, Chris 57
Messing, Debra 44, 51
Mestre, Adelaide 36
Metropolis, Nick 36
Metzman, Irving 20, 24, 42
Meyers, Gary Allen 32
Meyers, Jonathan Rhys 54
Michael Bell, Raymond 65
Michaels, Bert 20
Midler, Bette 35
Mihashi, Tatsuya 10
Milani, Mariella 62
Miles, Charles 32
Miles, Helen 40
Miles, Jenna 40
Miley, Peggy 33
Miller, Ebb 24
Miller, Helen 24, 25, 26
Miller, Jonny Lee 53
Miller, Michael 17
Miller, Sidney 14
Miller, Susan 15
Miller, Tracey Lynne 42
Milligan, Spencer 15
Millman, Gabriel 40, 44
Mims, Mary 20
Mineo, John 39, 40
Miner, Rachel 33

Mingalone, Dick 44, 46
Mintz, Eli 20
Miranti, Bob 20
Misner, Susan 40
Mitchell, Gregory 40
Mitchell, Radha 53
Mizrahi, Isaac 44, 48, 51
Mizuno, Kumi 10
Modell, Frank 20
Moinot, Michel 40
Mol, Gretchen 44, 46
Monday, Dick 46
Monica, Corbett 23
Montalbán, Carlos 13
Montané, Jaume 57
Moody, Jim 44
Moon, Michael 45
Moore, Dana 40
Moore, Demi 42
Moore, Gregory 35
Moore, Patience 33
Morales, Jacobo 13
Moran, Dan 39, 42, 44, 46, 50
Moran, Trevor 48
Morden, Roger 19
Morgenstern, Mindy 26
Morgenstern, Ross 26
Moroff, Madeline 20
Morris, A. Lee 44
Morris, Aubrey 16
Morris, Randy 67
Mortimer, Emily 54
Morton, Samantha 46
Mosberg, David 26
Mosca, Arsène 61
Moskowitz, Minnow 12
Mostel, Josh 26
Mostel, Zero 17
Moston, Murray 17
Mottola, Greg 44, 51
Mowat, Rick 44, 46
Mowery, Josh 46
Mr. Spoons 46
Mule Deer, Gary 18
Mulheren, Michael 50
Mullane, Dan 39
Muller, Didier 66
Muller, Ernst 31
Munk, Jonathan 18
Munk, Robert 20
Munna, Dax 29
Murphy, Andrew 24
Murphy, Michael 17, 19
Murphy, Micil 12
Murphy, Rosemary 28, 39

Murray, Chic 11
Murray, Marc 20
Murray, Michael 26
Musiker, Lee 32
Muti, Ornella 62
Myers, Troy 40
Myrin, Arden 42

N

Nader, Lindsay Michelle 58
Nakamaru, Tadao 10
Nakamura, Tetsu 10
Napolitan, Neil 20
Nappo, Monica 62
Nascarella, Arthur 50
Nauffts, Geoffrey 53
Nayber, Laurie 33
Neeson, Liam 36
Nelkin, Stacey 38
Nelligan, Kate 34
Nelson, Christopher 39
Nesbitt, James 54
Neuman, Joan 18, 20
Neustadt, Ted 44, 51, 64
Neuwirth, Bebe 44
Nevens, Paul 22
Newey, Simon 20
Newman, Joy 26
Newman, Roger 18
Nichols, Jenny 30, 32
Nickels, Rebecca 26, 35
Nicklaus, Jill 40
Nielsen, Kristine 48
Nikic, Fanda 48
Nimmo, Derek 11
Niven, David 11
Nocerino, Anthony 36
Nolan, Lloyd 25
Nolte, Nick 30
Noonan, Stephen 56
Norris, Mélanie 37
Norton, Edward 40
Nouel, Georges Édouard 66
Novello, Don 30
Novikoff, Rashel 18
Noyes, Tyler 41
Nozaki, Phillip 35
Nunes, Michaelah Noelle 67

O

O. Hobson, Verna 25
O'Brien, Frank 26
O'Brien, Vince 18

O'Connel, Robert 13
O'Donnell, Anthony 54, 55
O'Donoghue, Michael 19
O'Dowd, Mike 12
O'Hare, Denis 46
O'Neal, Patrick 30, 33
O'Neill, Suzann 33
O'Rourke, Mick 46
O'Shea, Milo 24
O'Steeen, Michael 40
O'Sullivan Farrow, Dylan 31, 32, 33
O'Sullivan, Maureen 25
O'Toole, Peter 10, 11
Oberton, Grady 67
Oberton, Josette 67
Occhino, Murphy 45
Oishi, Shirô 35
Oke, Alan 54
Okrent, Daniel 46
Oliveira, Joseph 67
Oliver, Rochelle 51
Olson, Aaron 67
Omaggio, Maria Rosaria 62
Onrubia, Cynthia 40
Ontiveros, Lupe 49
Orbach, Jerry 32
Orrach, Joe 40
Ortelli, Dyana 49
Orth, Zak 53, 57, 59
Ortiz, David 13
Ortiz, Steve 35
Ostaro 20
Otis, James 20
Ottenheimer, Albert 17, 18
Outhwaite, Tamzin 56
Overbey, Kellie 46
Owen, Meg Wynn 55

P

Pacheco, Rosemary 67
Pacho, Andrew 40
Pacifico, Camilla 62
Pagano, Joe 20
Page, Ellen 62
Page, Geraldine 19
Page, Victoria 20
Palagonia, Al 64
Palazzoni, Cristiana 62
Palermo, Chris 67
Palladino, Aleksa 44
Palminteri, Chazz 38
Pambieri, Giuseppe 62
Pantaeva, Irina 44
Pantano, Nicholas 23

Pantano, Rocco 23
Paolo, Gianni 67
Pappas, Mary 25
Pappé, Stuart 35
Paradis, Vanessa 65
Pardo, Don 26
Paredes, Jean 10
Parenti, Flavio 62
Paris, Renée 17
Paris, Robin Mary 18
Parish, Paula 46
Parker, Gloria 23
Parker, Mary-Louise 38
Parker, Sarah Jessica 41
Pasare, Georgette 39
Pasekoff, Marilyn 35
Pashalinski, Lola 46
Pasquesi, David 62
Patrick, Nicole 58
Paul, Tina 40
Paulson, William 23
Payne, Ruby 26
Peer, Beverly 25
Peet, Amanda 53
Peisner, Marvin 20
Pellegrino, Frank 37, 44
Pemberton, Steve 54
Penn, Sean 46
Penry-Jones, Rupert 54
Pepe, Neil 53
Peplowski, Ken 50
Peraza, Eulogio 13
Perez, Luis Martin 40
Pérez, Tigre 13
Perezic, Hamit 18
Perillán, Julio 57
Perlman, Itzhak 40
Perlman, Navah 40
Peron, Denise 16
Perri, Linda 42
Perroni, Jon 67
Perry, Roxanne 51
Persky, Marilyn 17
Persky, Stanley 45
Peters, Bernadette 33
Peterson, Nina Sonya 38
Pétin, Michèle 28
Petkoff, Robert 67
Petrolino, Dominick 20
Petrucelli, Rick 18, 24
Pettet, Joanna 11
Pettet, Kristen 40
Philbin, Regis 14
Philippe, Andre 35
Phillips, Ethan 67

Phillips, Lou Diamond 49
Phoenix, Joaquin 67
Picard, Connie 36
Picetti, Lou 15, 18
Picker, Si 42
Piddock, Jim 59
Piedimonte, Andrea 40
Pierce, Wendell 37
Pietri, Frank 40
Pilavin, Barbara 49
Pill, Alison 60, 62
Pine, Haley 67
Pine, Larry 44, 48, 53
Pinkins, Tonya 65
Pinto, Freida 59
Pipgras, Christine 48
Pissors, Wolfgang 66
Pistilli, Carl 23
Pitt, Myla 32
Pittu, David 67
Placksin, Sally 46
Plana, Tony 49
Pleasance, Donald 34
Plimpton, Martha 29
Plum, Paula 67
Poivre, Annette 10
Pole, Frances 20
Polen, Sarah 51
Polenz, Robert 33
Polk, James Duane 35
Pollack, Sydney 36
Ponce, Ramon 35
Ponella, Mike 45
Poor, Bray 39
Popa, Robert 67
Pope, Ralph 42, 44, 46, 52
Portal, Robert 59
Porter, Beth 16
Porter, Joan 17
Portman, Natalie 40
Portnow, Richard 26
Posey, Parker 67
Posner, Russell 65
Postrel, Leo 24, 25
Poterlot, Stéphane 61
Pourfar, Susan 67
Prentiss, Paula 10
Prestianni, Steven Dominic 35
Preston, Carrie 57
Previn, Daisy 25
Previn, Soon-Yi 25, 35
Price, Molly 46
Pridham, Alyssa 53
Prince, Daisy 40, 42, 44
Princess Fatosh 13

Procoli, Alessandro 62
Puente, Tito 26
Punch, Lucy 59

Q

Quayle, Anna 11
Quayle, Anthony 14
Quesada, Juan 57
Questel, Mae 31
Quidjada, Francisco 44
Quigley, Don 24
Quigley, Pearce 59
Quinones, Fernando 35

R

Rabinowitz, Hannah 26
Rabourdin, Olivier 60
Radburn, Veronica 18
Rae, Charlotte 13
Rafart, Carlos 41
Raffaelli, Suzanne 37
Raffone, Antoinette 23
Raflo, Paula 20
Raft, George 11
Ragaini, Robert 40
Rainone, Gabriele 62
Rains, Jessica 15
Raison, Miranda 54
Rampino, Antonio 62
Rampling, Charlotte 20
Ramsay, Remak 17, 34
Ramsey, Allan 56
Randall, Tony 14
Randazzo, Steven 36, 37, 39, 44
Ranone, Maggie 23
Rapaport, Michael 39, 48
Raphael, Marilyn 44
Rasche, David 19
Rath, Tina 55
Rathbone, Hugh 56
Rayson, Benjamin 20, 24
Re, Marina 67
Rebhorn, James 34
Redfield, Adam 21
Redgrave, Lynn 14
Redmond, Marge 37
Reed, Darryl Alan 46
Reed, Tracy 11
Regan, Molly 31, 38
Reggio, Ariella 62
Reichman, Stanley 32
Reidy, Joseph 42
Reilly, John C. 34

Reiner, Rob 38
Reno, James 38
Renzulli, Frank 23
Resnick, Eli 22
Resnick, Floyd 42
Reynolds, Burt 14
Reynolds, Gary 23
Reynolds, Herb 23
Ribustello, Anthony J. 52
Ricci, Christina 52
Richards, Adrian 20
Richardson, Jack 36
Richardson, Jerome 46
Richman, Sandy 23
Richmond, George 56
Richmond, Krissy 40
Rickman, Allen Lewis 65
Riedel, Lutz 43
Riehle, Richard 34
Rifkin, Ron 36, 37
Rigano, Joe 46, 51
Riggs III, Charles 20
Riggs, Geoffrey 20
Rigillo, Mariano 62
Rigsby, Gordon 36
Riley, Penny 11
Ringwald, Molly 28
Risley, Ann 20
Rizzo, Michael 31
Roa, Andrew 49
Roberts, Judith 20
Roberts, Julia 40
Roberts, Ken 26, 38
Roberts, Lenny 40
Roberts, Phyllis 56
Roberts, Tony 15, 18, 20, 21, 25, 26
Robin, Tucker 39
Robinson, Bartlett 15
Robinson, Jay 14
Robinson, Max 34
Rocco, Marina 62
Rockwell, Sam 44
Rodriguez, Valente 49
Rogers, Ingrid 45
Roland, Jeanne 11
Rolf, Frederick 40, 42, 44
Rolland, Sonia 60
Rollins, Bob 23
Rollins, Etta 23
Rollins, Jack 20, 23
Rollis, Robert 10
Romano, Christy 40
Ronconi, Roberta 62
Rosario, Willie 40
Roscoe, Gary 67

Rose, Adam 42
Rose, Mickey 10, 12, 13
Rose, Minna 35
Rose, Norman 16, 17, 26
Rose, Quincy 53
Rose, Skip 44
Rosen, Herschel 23, 31
Rosenblatt, Martin 18, 26, 31
Rosenfeld, Moishe 21
Rosenfield, Ben 67
Rosenstein, Jamie 67
Rosotti, Betty 23
Ross, Stanley 15
Ross, Yolonda 58
Rossett, Alan 16
Rossini, Anna Teresa 62
Rostain, François 60
Roth Haberle, Stephanie 32, 42, 51, 53
Roth, Tim 40
Rothman, John 20, 22, 24
Rothschild, Elizabeth 22
Routh, Jonathan 11
Rowlands, Gena 29
Rubens, Herbert 41
Rubin, Christopher 64
Ruehl, Mercedes 26
Ruggiero, Lou 31
Rugoff, Ruth 20
Ruinsky, Robin 20
Rush, Deborah 22, 24
Ruskin, Dan 18
Ruskin, Shimen 16
Russel, Percival 16
Russell, Stewart 35
Rutherford, Max 64
Ryan, Bridgit 31
Rydell, Mark 51
Ryder, Winona 44
Ryland, Jonathan 59

S

Sabatasso, Halie 67
Sabaté, Sílvia 57
Sacharoff, Hope W. 38
Safra, Jaqui 20, 26
Saint-Bris, Richard 10
Sakai, Sachio 10
Saks, Gene 42
Salinger, Diane 33
Salmon, Colin 54
Salom, Ricard 57
Salt, Jennifer 15
Salvail, Eve 44
Sanchez, Ref 14

Sanders, Annette 40
Sanders, Chris 16
Sandke, Randy 50
Sanford, Nadia 32
Sanson, Kathy 40
Sarafian, Richard C. 49
Sarsgaard, Peter 64
Sastri, Lina 62
Sauchelli Jr., Alfred 46
Saunders, Nicholas 13
Saviola, Camille 23, 24, 34
Saxon, Carolyn 46, 48
Scamarcio, Riccardo 62
Sceusa, Anna 23
Schaake, Katrin 10
Schaale, Gerald 43
Schaeffer, Rebecca 26
Scheller, Damion 19
Schenck, John 29
Schiano, Marina 20
Schindler, George 31
Schmidt, Benno 25, 36
Schmidtberger, Mary 44, 51
Schneider, David 55
Schneider, Romy 10
Schnurr, Vikki 40
Schoenfeld, Gerald 23
Schreiber, Liev 41, 65
Schreiber, Pablo 57
Schuck, John 50
Schull, Rebecca 32
Schultz, Armand 58
Schultz, Carol 29
Schumann, Katja 33
Schuppert, Geoff 67
Schwartzberg, Antonette 44
Schwimmer, David 49
Scooler, Zvee 16
Scott, Jill 65
Scott, Rob 25
Scoular, Angela 11
Seaman, Milton 24
Sechler, Craig 39
Seganti, Paolo 40
Seldes, Marian 51
Sellars, Peter 28
Sellers, Peter 10, 11
Selya, John 40
Semer, Katelyn 67
Senerchia, Eva 67
Serna, Pepe 49
Serra, Raymond 19, 24
Serrato, Ilaria 62
Servitto, Matt 53
Setterfield, Valda 39, 40

Sevigny, Chloë 53
Sexton, Dora 67
Seydoux, Léa 60
Sfinias, Yanni 37
Shaiman, Marc 35
Shamos, Jeremy 66
Shankin, Bobby 42
Shaud, Grant 43
Shaw, Dickson 25
Shaw, Vinessa 53
Shawn, Wallace 19, 26, 34, 50, 53
Sheen, Michael 60
Shelley, Joshua 17
Shenkel, Leslie 44
Shepherd, Cybill 33
Sherman, Larry 35
Sherman, Martin 26
Sherrill, Martha 20, 24
Shevlin, Jean 24
Sheybal, Vladek 11
Shimerman, Armin 20
Shire, Talia 30
Shore, Nancy Ellen 67
Short, Bobby 25
Shrog, Maurice 20, 23, 26
Shue, Elisabeth 42
Shulman, Constance 46
Shultz, Philip 26
Sietz, Adam 44
Sillah, Salimatou 65
Sills, Paul 29
Silver, Robert 34
Simmonds, Stanley 22
Simmons, J.K. 44
Simon, Paul 18
Simowitz, Garrett 32
Sims, Mark 66
Sinclaire, Jhennah 67
Singer, Stephen 41
Sinopoli, Anthony 48
Sirico, Tony 38, 39, 40, 42, 44
Siroux, Sébastien 66
Siverio, Manny 52
Slade, Melissa 20
Slater, John J. 17
Sloan, Tina 44, 50
Small, Marya 15
Smee, Keith 56
Smiar, Brian 34
Smith Cameron, J. 39
Smith, Brooke 53
Smith, C.A.R. 16
Smith, Claudia 62
Smith, Derek 32
Smith, Fred 16

Smith, Kurtwood 34
Smith, Leslie 20
Smits, Theodore R. 22
Snell, Don 33
Sokol, Marilyn 17
Sokolow, Ethel 12
Solar, Cory 46
Solas, Paul 61
Solli, Sergio 62
Sommer, Inken 43
Sommer, Josef 17, 34
Sommer, Ted 50
Sommers, Barbara 10
Sonnenberg, Maurice 44, 48, 50, 51, 52, 57, 60, 64
Sonnenschein, Klaus 43
Sontag, Susan 22
Sorvino, Mira 39
Soto, José 41
Sotos, Tony 32
Soulier, Yannick 61
Spagnuolo, Filomena 20
Spiegel, Howard 42
Spielberg, David 33
Spielvogel, Laurent 60
Spiner, Brent 20
Spivak, Alice 20, 29
Sponholz, Kuno 22, 26
Spoto, Yves-Antoine 60
Sprague, Michael 46
Squibb, June 33
Stallone, Sylvester 13, 43
Standing, John 55
Stanford, Aaron 51
Stapleton, Joe 67
Stapleton, Maureen 19
Stark, Graham 11
Starr, Mike 26, 31
Stebner, Greg 34
Steenburgen, Mary 21
Stein, Dennis 46
Stein, Margaret Sophie 38
Stein, Phil 38
Steiner, Leo 23
Steinfink, Iryn 20
Stern, Daniel 20, 25
Stettner, Dave 42
Stevens, Fisher 52
Stewart, Paul Anthony 34
Stiers, David Ogden 29, 34, 39, 40, 50
Stirling, Richard 55
Stoll, Corey 60
Stone, Emma 66, 67
Stone, Sharon 20, 43, 49, 65
Storm, Howard 12, 23
Stout, Mary 46

Stram, Henry 67
Strange, Meghan 38
Strasun, Gabrielle 20
Streatfield, Geoffrey 54
Streep, Meryl 19
Strickland, KaDee 52
Stritch, Elaine 28, 48
Struffolino, David 67
Stuhlbarg, Michael 64
Sturgis, William 25
Styles, Bernie 18
Suárez, Miguel 13
Subor, Michel 10
Sullivan, Heather 29
Sullivan, Michael-Vaughn 33
Summo, Joseph 20
Sun, Sabine 10
Sunjata, Daniel 53
Sutherland, Kiefer 49
Sutherland, Ted 65
Sutton, Dolores 32
Swanson, Lynn 62
Swanson, Michael Steven 67
Swarts, Terry Lee 26
Sweda, Fred 29
Sweeney, Matthew 44
Swerdlow, Stanley 22
Syal, Meera 55, 59
Symington, Donald 17, 18, 39

T

Taglioni, Alice 61
Tahan, Charlie 64
Takada, Hidehiko 35
Takahashi, Reiko 51
Tallarida, Alessandro 62
Tanaka, Lino 67
Taschini, Antonio 62
Tassell, Gustave 20
Tatum, Marianne 22
Taylor, Adrienne 67
Taylor, Andy 41
Taylor, Bernard 16
Taylor, Billy 33
Taylor, Elaine 11
Taylor, Holland 33
Taylor, Joseph Lyle 52
Taylor, Linda 37
Taylor, Myra Lucretia 40
Tedesco, Tony 32, 45
Telford, Jo 38, 40
Telford, Zoe 54
Tempesta, Carl „CJ" 67
Tenenbaum, Irwin 25

Tennenhouse, Robert 20
Terban, Marvin 32, 33
Terzis, Greg 67
Textor, Terry 40
Thayer, Brynn 64
The 39 Steps 25
Theron, Charlize 44, 50
Thierry, Clément 16
Thiessen, Tiffani 51
Thomas, Ray Anthony 41
Thomas, Vaneese 40
Thomas, Vanessa 33
Thompson, Margaret 24
Thomson, Colin 64
Thomson, Margaret 26
Thurman, Uma 46
Tiberi, Alessandro 62
Tice, David 24
Ticotin, Nancy 40
Tijerina, Cecilia 49
Tilly, Jennifer 38
Tilvern, Alan 16
Timoney, Bill 39
Tjan, Willie 24
Toa, Guo 55
Toback, James 33
Tobin, Matthew 17
Tognazzi, Gianmarco 62
Tolan, Peter 33
Tolkan, James 16
Toma, Judy 51
Tomlin, Lily 34
Tong, Kathy 64
Toorvald, Sven 39
Torlage, Leigh 38
Tormey, John 50
Torres, Robert 44
Torterello, Gilda 23
Touchard, Michel 20
Toueg, Maurice 26
Towey, John Madden 29
Towler, Laurine 48
Trebor, Robert 24
Treger, Martina 43
Troobnick, Eugene 42
Trowbridge, Jean 22
Troy, Michael P. 34
Trueman, Paula 18, 22
Trump, Donald 44
Truro, Victor 19, 20, 36
Tucci, Stanley 42
Tucker, Michael 24, 26
Tudisco, Joseph 44
Tuffy, Nolan 39
Tuminello, Sal 26

Tupper, Loretta 18, 24
Turca, Tony 23
Turco, Tony 36
Turek, Ron 34
Turley, Michelle 36
Turturro, Aida 37, 44, 65
Turturro, Diego 65
Turturro, John 25, 65
Tyler, Dana 48
Tyzack, Margaret 54, 55
Tzavaras, Nicholas 53

U

Ullman, Tracey 38, 48
Ulmschneider, Craig 44
Umbers, Mark 56
Urbaniak, James 46
Uzan, Emanuelle 60

V

Vaché, Warren 32
Valenti, J. P. 67
Vallier, Helen 16
van der Wal, Frederique 44
Van Dyck, Jennifer 38
Van Valkenburg, Eric 20
Van Wagner, Peter 51
Vanasse, Karine 60
Vance, Kenny 19, 20, 32, 36
Vandenburgh, Craig 23
Vanderloo, Mark 44
Vandis, Titos 14
Vassilopoulos, Dimitri 20, 22, 26
Ventimiglia, Johnny 38
Venuta, Benay 38
Verdon, Gwen 33
Vergara, Sofia 65
Vernoff, Kaili 46, 50
Vernon, Howard 10, 16
Vestunis, Dennis 34
Vezina, George 67
Viano, Franck 56
Vicario, Margherita 62
Victor, Rene 35
Vidal, Lisa 39
Vienna, Christine 65
Villone, Nancy 67
Viterelli, Joe 38
Viva 15
Viviani, Joe 35
Vivona, Jerome 40
Vochecowizc, Liz 26
Vohs, Frank 18

Volner, Ruth 18
Von Bargen, Daniel 34
Von Berg, Peter 24
von Haselberg, Sophie 67
von Sydow, Max 25
Vuillermoz, Michel 60

W

Wakabayashi, Akiko 10
Walden, Robert 14
Walken, Christopher 18, 43
Walker, Natalie 59
Walker, Robert 40
Wallem, Linda 33
Walsh, J. T. 25
Walter, Tracey 18
Warden, Jack 28, 38, 39
Warren, Brian 35
Warren, Joseph 35
Warrilow, David 26
Warwick, Margaretta 18
Waters, John 46
Waterston, Sam 19, 25, 28, 32
Wattis, Richard 11
Watts, Naomi 59
Weaver, Jacki 66
Weaver, Sigourney 18
Webber, Mark 51
Weber, David 24
Weddell, Mimi 24
Weil, Bob 23
Weis, Gary 19
Weiss, Barry 20
Weist, Dwight 22, 26
Welch, Christopher Evan 57, 58
Weller, Peter 39
Welles, Orson 11
Wells, John 11
Welsh, Kenneth 26, 29
Wess, Frank Wellington 46
West, H.E. 14
Weston, Celia 44
Weston-Moran, Kim 33
Wettenhall, Simon 46
Weyand, Ron 34
Wheeler, Ira 25, 26, 28, 31, 33, 34, 36, 37, 48, 50
Whitaker, Jill 29
White, Daisy 49
Whitehead, Martha 20
Whiting, Richard A. 22
Whitlock, Isiah 40
Whitlock, Lee 56
Whymark, Patricia 54
Wickham, Jeffry 55

Wier, David 18
Wiest, Dianne 24, 25, 26, 28, 38
Wilcox, Pamela Figueiredo 67
Wilcox, Paula 55
Wilder, Gene 14
Wilkins, Ted 46
Wilkinson, Ashley H. 40
Wilkinson, Tom 56
Wilks, Cindy 48
Williams, Gigi 45
Williams, Glenn 16
Williams, James 46
Williams, Robin 42
Williams, Treat 51
Williamson, Matt 33
Wilmes, Gary 67
Wilrich, Rudolph 17
Wilson, Chuck 50
Wilson, Mary Louise 22
Wilson, Owen 60
Wilton, Penelope 54
Winant, Bruce 39
Wiseman, Debra 38
Witkin, Jacob 16
Wolchok, Robert Lloyd 51
Wolf, Daniel 42
Wolfangle, Karla 48
Wollasch, Peter 66
Wood, Evan Rachel 58
Wood, Frank 48
Wood, John 24
Woodruff, Largo 20
Woods, Carol 46
Woods, Dana 49
Woolgar, Fenella 55, 59
Wright, Amy 20
Wright, Jeffrey 44
Wright, Maggie 10
Wright, Mary Catherine 44
Wright, Rebecca 20
Wynn, Lisa 67

Y

Yanovsky, Zal 10
Yuk, Henry 26
Yulin, Harris 29
Yusuf, Osman 10

Z

Zaks, Jerry 32, 36
Zannella, Michael 20
Zard, Patrick 66
Zaremby, Justin 32

Zeisler, Mark 67
Zenor, Suzanne 15
Zhang, Chun Long 35
Zimmerman, Grace 32
Zion, Rabbi Joel 32
Zoffoli, Marta 62

Zoldessy, Brian 20
Zolten, Diane 23
Zoubok, Boris 21
Zucchini, Alessio 62
Zussin, Victoria 20, 24
Zwingel, Jürgen 66